DON'T ASK MY NAME

DON'T ASK MY NAME

A Hidden Child's Tale of Survival

ERIKA HECHT

EAST END PRESS
BRIDGEHAMPTON • NEW YORK

This book is to honor the memory of the children who did not survive the Holocaust and is dedicated to those who lived and had the courage to confront the trauma of their survival.

DON'T ASK MY NAME

Copyright © 2021 by Erika Hecht

Published by
EAST END PRESS
Bridgehampton, NY

Hardcover ISBN: 978-1-7345268-3-7
eBook ISBN: 978-1-7345268-4-4

FIRST EDITION

Book and Jacket Design by Pauline Neuwirth, Neuwirth & Associates, Inc.

Manufactured in the United States of America
10 9 8 7 6 5 4 3 2 1

ACKNOWLEDGMENTS

This book could not have come into existence without the support, enthusiasm, and contribution of several committed people.

First and foremost, I want to acknowledge my daughter, Marion, who has been the most supportive and encouraging person since I first began to talk about my experiences. The more stories she heard, the more convinced she became about the necessity for me to write them all down. She accompanied me to Hungary on my "roots trip" in 1993, which helped me verify all of my memories and was further confirmation that this book had to be written. She remains to this day my most ardent supporter.

Another person without whose expertise and cooperation this book could not have happened is my friend Anne McCormack, a supportive and understanding soul, whose ability with the computer transformed my handwritten stories into a manuscript. It was a long, sometimes difficult process, but she never lost faith in my ability to finish the book. Her patience was endless. As the years went by, she was even able to read my handwriting.

Andrew Skonka has also been a continuing support in many aspects of my life and was always available to help with the technical aspects of putting the book together.

There were other helpful and positive influences over the years, the most notable being the Ashawagh Hall Writing Group, which I belonged to for many years. We met every week over the winters, reading from our manuscripts and receiving criticism and inspiration from our very accomplished peers.

CONVERSION

· 1937 ·

"You have to behave," my mother says. "You have to be very, very good." Her voice is serious, low, and threatening, and her grip on my hand is firm as she pulls me along with her. We are walking toward a big yellow building. "This is the church," she says. "Watch your step," she says, and, "What are you staring at?" when I stumble on the steps leading to the church's entrance. Mother picks me up and impatiently carries me the rest of the way up the stairs. Somehow, I know and understand that she is afraid. I am three-and-a-half years old.

We go inside. It is dark and smells of burning wood, like our stove at home when the fire is about to go out. Many candles are burning near the walls, but it is still too dark to make out the pictures hanging above them. I am cold and frightened and I tell my mother that I want to leave. "No," she says, "no, no, no." I start to cry, but to no avail. She continues to pull me along with her toward the front. "The Pater is waiting for us," she says. "Now stop crying, don't ask any questions, and be a good little girl."

"Where are the birds?" I ask as we pass what looks like a birdbath on the way to the front. It looks exactly like the one in my cousin Marika's garden. Mother stops for a moment and then she says, "That is holy water. Now you must really be quiet or else!"

The Pater wears a long black dress. He stands on the stairs in front of a railing. I can see two boys standing behind him and wonder why they are wearing nightshirts. The Pater starts to speak to my mother slowly in a low voice. He is very serious. I cannot understand anything he is saying. Mother is listening, nodding, and talking to the Pater without paying any attention to me. I am getting bored. I say, "I want to go home. I'm hungry," but she continues to listen only to the priest. Suddenly, my mother kneels down on the step in front of him. Why is she doing that? Is there some dirt on the floor she wants to clean? Did she see a bug? No, she is still looking at the priest, listening. I am so frightened that I start to cry again. When the priest puts something in my mother's mouth, my crying turns into a wail, and I continue to wail even as we are leaving the church.

Outside the sun is shining. It is warm, so why is my mother shaking? Two ladies, her friends, are waiting for us. They are speaking to her, comforting her, telling her that everything will be all right. They tell me to be a good girl, to stop crying, but I cannot. Mother lifts me up, and I see that she too is crying. She continues to carry me as we walk away from the church, bouncing me up and down to comfort me, or maybe herself. She keeps repeating the same words louder and louder: "We are Christians now. We are Catholics. We are safe. The bastards cannot hurt us. Nobody can hurt us. We are Christians."

NEW YORK

• 1991 •

As I leaf through *New York* magazine on a sunny Sunday afternoon in Montreal, the picture of a young girl disrupts my musings. She looks like me, or at least what I must have looked like in 1945 when the war ended. The hairdo, strict and orderly; the skirt, the hem just below the knee; and her serious expression staring into the camera brings to mind one particular photograph taken of me at that time. The picture in the magazine accompanies an article describing a forthcoming conference in New York, the very first conference for "The Hidden Children of the Holocaust." The article gives a vivid explanation of the term "Hidden Children." It refers to Jewish children who were provided false identities and survived World War II as Christians. The lies these children were obliged to tell and the secrets they had to keep accompanied them the rest of their lives, and according to the article, some fifty years later, the now-adult children are finally starting to talk. I have never before seen anything in print about Hidden Children. Reading the article moves me deeply. The girl in the picture was a Hidden Child, and until now, almost fifty years later, she has never talked about how the memories of her experiences have influenced her life. Nor have I.

My peaceful afternoon is shattered. Memories I didn't find necessary to remember are starting to invade my consciousness. Although I was converted to Catholicism with my mother in 1937, when I was three and a half, by 1942 the anti-Jewish laws in Hungary had changed. Our conversion no longer exempted us from being Jewish. By 1942, to be exempt from the anti-Jewish laws, it was required to document four non-Jewish grandparents. Although we were Catholics, my family had to find other ways of posing as non-Jews in order to survive Nazi persecution. We were fortunately able to acquire false identities through fake birth certificates and other pertinent documents and move to a village where we were not known, so that we could live as non-Jews. I was required from a very young age to lie and to keep secrets in order to survive.

I want to know more about the conference. I call the number at the end of the article and find out that it is to be held at the Marriott Marquis Hotel in New York City at the end of May over a long weekend. The program consists of several workshops led by professional therapists, all survivors themselves. They are expecting approximately three hundred people.

ON ARRIVAL AT THE hotel, I learn that the actual number of par- ticipants has risen to close to sixteen hundred. Fortunately, the Marriott can open more conference rooms to accommodate the swelling numbers. When I look around, I see a vibrant, successful-looking group of people, mostly my age. Many have shown up in person to check out what's going on, suspicious of what sounds like an intrusion into their long suppressed "hidden past." Judging by the time it takes most of them to fill out their registration forms, they are still cautious about sharing their identity.

The first workshop I attend is called "Christian or Jew?" and in spite of the question's validity for me, I am not even tempted to participate. I want to observe and learn. I need time. The next one is called "I Never Had a Childhood." It is conducted by a well-known New York psychotherapist and survivor named Magda. She is from Budapest, where I am from as well. She is a tall, impressive woman, walking back and forth in front of the group. It seems as if her eyes do not leave my face, never turning or moving far away enough to lose sight of me. "What does she want from me?" I think. "Why is she staring at me? Why is she not staring at anybody else?" I am uncomfortable and consider leaving the room, but I would have to cross in front of her on the way to the door. I do not want to be ill-mannered, so I stay.

A woman from Poland is telling her story. When she was three years old and Jews were already being deported to camps, kindly Christian people—acquaintances of her parents—took her in, converted her to Christianity, and kept her as their own child. She was seven when her parents fortunately returned after the war. She did not recognize them. Tragically, she did not want to rejoin them, nor did the people who saved her want to give her up. Her story is heart-wrenching and she herself is crying. Most of the people in the room are crying as well. But I am not. I will not let anybody else's sadness move me to tears.

Some of the details of her story remind me of my own background. Since the end of the war, I was never encouraged to speak of the particulars of my survival. "Lucky girl," I was told. "You were too young to remember. It is better to forget and get back to *normal* life." I was eleven in 1945, but I was treated as if I had come alive only when the war was over. Later, my husband, children, and friends knew only broad outlines of my history. No one ever asked about any of the specifics of what had happened to me during the war—not even my husband or his family. No one seemed to want to know, nor was I eager to share, realizing that it would be depressing and shameful and would cause a lot of pain. While listening to this woman's tearful account, I am determined to honor my fifty years of silence. My hidden childhood had to remain hidden.

The therapist's staring continues and becomes even more intense, while Magda is sharing some of her own story. She survived the Holocaust in Budapest hiding with some Christian relatives, together with her mother and brother. They had fake documents according to which they were Catholics (like me). Magda continues to say a few words about her brother and about the manner in which he had died—starvation. Her words are simple and eloquent, yet convey the intense pain and anguish of her loss.

I feel myself choking on the tears I try to suppress, but I am not going to cry. Magda, still looking at me, addresses me suddenly with something of a sarcastic smile. "But you, my dear, you had a pleasant childhood, or did you not?" I do not answer, and she continues to challenge me. "You had a loving mother, doting grandparents, lots and lots of toys, lovely clothes—an adoring father—and of course—*enough food.*"

I can't help myself. I yell, "Stop it! How can you say that? Why do you, of all people, want to make me remember?" As I am saying these things, I start to sob. Under her relentless gaze and due to her selfless sharing, I lose my ability to remain silent. I start to talk about some of the experiences I had as a hidden Jewish child during the war. I cannot stop talking and crying. I am still sobbing when the session ends.

During the next few days of the conference, the seating at dinner is arranged by country of origin and year of birth, as the experience of being hidden varied greatly according to the country you were born in and the year the persecutions started in that particular country. There is a lot of talking and a lot more crying. I am surprised by how sharp my memories are and how incredibly painful. Exchanging our stories, the similarities of our suffering, and the miracle of our survival brings us closer and closer together.

Over the next couple of days in workshops and at dinner tables, a lot of stories are told and a lot of tears are shed. Yet, sharing is totally liberating. "Do you have any cousins?" somebody will ask. I have only two left out of six. Others have none. The most important question waiting for an answer is: "Are you Christian or are you Jew?"

I tell the story of my husband and I visiting Europe as tourists. We went to some churches in Italy and Spain. "I could not," I recall, "walk into a Catholic church without dipping my fingers into holy water, making the sign of the cross, and genuflecting. The first time I did this, my Jewish husband was appalled and told me never to do it again. But I could not help myself. Although I had a Jewish identity through my marriage by then, I still felt the need to honor my Catholic education."

My group of soulmates understands exactly what I am talking about. The identification I feel with everyone's stories is a very welcome and undexpected surprise. I feel an all-encompassing sense of validation, of acceptance, of compassion, and of love. At the age of fifty-seven, I finally feel that I am becoming closer to my true self. My need to remember and talk becomes stronger and stronger as the conference draws to an end.

On the final night, I call my daughter, Marion, who is living in Florida. I tell her that I am ready to talk about my childhood. Her reaction is immediate, positive, and astounding to me. "I can't believe that I might find out about the part of your life that has never been talked about," she says. "There always was a dark hole in my heart," she continues, "where your history should have taken up some space." Her insatiable curiosity and sustained interest in my stories become a motivating force for me to pursue talking about more and more of my memories.

As a result of the conference, groups are established in many countries. Hidden Children are finally coming out of hiding. Great changes take place in the lives of many people. In the next few years, conferences are held as far away as Melbourne, Australia, and as close as New Jersey. I, together with many other participants of that first unforgettable conference in New York, go on to accept speaking engagements in various educational institutions teaching and sharing our stories and history of the Second World War and the Holocaust.

Sharing the memories of my past is healing for me. Sometimes when I talk about a particularly gruesome or sad scene, Marion says, "Write it down." Slowly, I begin to make notes and I become less intimidated by my own stories. Hopefully, they will add to society's understanding of this particular time in history and the Holocaust and contribute to the realization that the evil committed against humanity must never happen again.

What follows are some of the stories of my life before, during, and after the war.

BOOK ONE

"I will not set foot into a Jewish church.
It's a mortal sin."

CHAPTER ONE

BUDAPEST

• 1939–1943 •

"I DO NOT LIKE kindergarten. I am not going."

Grandmother Adél is angry. "You have to go," she says. "There are many children there you like to play with." I start to cry and stamp my feet. "I'm not going, I'm not going, I'm not going."

"Stop the tantrum," she says. "You have to go."

Juliska, the housekeeper, is standing there in her jacket ready to escort me to kindergarten as she has done since I started school. When I see her, I know it is time to leave and I cry even harder. "I hate the teacher. She is mean, mean, mean."

Grandmother Adél decides to take me herself. On the way, she wants to know what the teacher has done that is so mean. I tell her that yesterday, I wanted to go to the bathroom but we were already wearing our coats to go and play in the yard. The teacher said, "We are going outside now. You have to wait."

"I can't wait," I said. "She didn't listen to me and I had to go outside. I tried to hold it but I couldn't. I started to smell. When we came in, I told her that my pants were full."

"You'll be going home soon," she said. "They'll take care of it."

"I was really uncomfortable. I couldn't even walk. Juliska carried me and took care of it when we got home. You were out and I didn't dare to tell you when you came home because I was afraid you would be angry that I made in my pants."

When Grandmother Adél and I get to school, I hang up my coat and sit down at the table that is supposed to be my place while she talks to the teacher. I can tell that she is getting angry. Then she gets my coat from the hook, takes my hand, and says, "We're leaving." As we walk home, she tells me, "You don't have to go back. I don't like the teacher either. You're right. She is mean and maybe she is an anti-Semite."

My grandmother's name is Adél Ács; my grandfather is Béla Ács. I live with them on Vilmos Császár Körút 23 in Budapest, Hungary. I'm five and a half years old and I have to know all of this in case we get stopped and questioned by the police. My grandparents look Jewish and sometimes the police stop and question people who look Jewish.

I like my Grandmother Adél. I am happy to stay with her and follow her around and do the things we always do. She gives me lessons on how to do things right. She teaches me to thread a needle, to darn socks, and to sew. I know how to crochet little things, like doilies, and I know how to knit a long scarf with big needles. In the kitchen she lets me help her and Juliska when they cook. I stand on a footstool and stir the potatoes or other things that are boiling because I know how to be very careful. She stands next to me to help me.

When Grandmother Adél goes to the market, I go with her. I like it when we go to buy a goose. We go to a store that sells chickens and geese. They have all been cleaned and prepared and are lined up on shelves all around. "When you buy a goose, you have to be sure that the liver is big," she says. "Watch me." As we approach a line of geese laid out on a low counter, she removes a hat pin from her hat and proceeds to pierce one of the geese at approximately where the liver should end. "If the pin comes out clean, it is not a good goose. The liver is too small," she says. I love goose liver. I have it often, fried on a fresh roll for a snack.

I live with my grandparents because after my father, Henry, left, when I was three years old, my mother had to go to work. We used to have an apartment that had a courtyard. Father moved out and we had to move too. Mother now sells beautiful leather gloves and expensive scarves and silk stockings in a small store in Kígyó utca. She now has an apartment near the school that I will attend. The address is Károly Körút 26, and the apartment is on the third floor. Our phone number is 383041. She takes me there sometimes and shows me the room that will be mine when I move back with her when I start first grade. I am excited about that but also sad and worried because I love living with my grandparents. Grandmother Adél spends the whole day with me. My mother would never do that.

Grandma tells me that my parents are now divorced but they don't hate each other. She likes my father and never says anything bad about him. They talk a lot to each other when he comes to pick me up on Sundays. My father and I go to visit my other grandmother, Kato néni. Sometimes my Aunt Hedi is there with my cousins Zsuzsa and Jutka. The food is very good there too, and there are always some of my favorites, like paprika chicken with dumplings.

Supper with my grandparents Ács is nice. We are kosher. Our suppers are *milchig*, which means no meat. Grandfather's supper is the same every night: two soft-boiled eggs eaten out of an egg cup and two large slices of fresh country bread, buttered and cut into long strips. I love to watch him cut off the top of the egg with one quick motion of the knife and dunk a strip of bread into the egg yolk. He lines up the other strips of bread like soldiers on his plate. He calls them two opposing armies and explains how one of them will make certain moves to win the battle. He was an officer in World War I and enjoys telling me about that too. I love my grandfather's war stories.

Some mornings when he is not working, he likes to take me for a walk. Not far from the apartment, there is a butcher shop that sells sandwiches. We stop there and Béla bácsi (as everybody calls him) orders ham and cheese on a buttered roll. "Two of them, please," he says. We sit on the back stoop of the building and eat the delicious sandwiches. "Make sure you do not tell your grandmother," says Grandfather Béla. "As long as no crumbs go home with us, the house remains kosher." He usually finishes my sandwich, which is too big for me, and makes sure that my clothes don't carry telltale signs of our misdeed. I like the sandwiches and I love having secrets with Grandfather.

One day he gets sick with pneumonia. When he feels somewhat better, he is sent to a sanatorium in Fiume to recuperate. Mother is over for dinner one night when a phone call comes from Fiume. A doctor tells Mother to come quickly because my grandfather is dying. There is a lot of carrying on about how to get there fast. But soon, there is another phone call from the doctor to tell us that Grandfather is fine. He had a severe allergic reaction to lobster, but he is much better and he is going to fully recover. Grandmother Adél is sobbing. "Lobster is one of the forbidden foods of the Jewish faith. Why did he eat that?" she bemoans. I think that I am the only one who has seen Béla bácsi eat forbidden food before, like our ham sandwiches. But I don't say anything. After Grandfather has recovered and comes home, every time the story of his getting sick from eating lobster is talked about, he looks at me and winks with a big smile.

Mother has dinner with us most nights. She and my grandfather talk about politics and worry about the war reaching
Hungary. I want to know if there will be opposing armies when
the war comes, like my grandfather's soldier games. But they
don't want to talk about that. What they are talking about is how
to stay safe when the Germans come closer and Jews are perse-
cuted and deported like in other countries.

Grandmother joins the conversation and changes the subject
as she asks Mother, "Did you tell Erika about Pista?"

Mother looks at me and says, "Did I tell you yet? I don't remember if I did or not."

"No, you didn't tell me anything. I know Pista is your boyfriend. I have met him once or twice and he was nice. He made
funny jokes."

"He is going to live with us," she tells me.

"Are you going to give him my room?"

"Of course not," says my mother. "He is moving in with us
and will stay in my room. You like Pista, don't you?"

"Yes, I do," I say. And I don't know why but I start to cry.

"Don't be a child. Stop crying," says Mother.

Mother does not like me to cry. I know that but I'm sad. Pista
is nice, but he is going to live with us and he's not my father.

When first grade starts, I move to the apartment with Mother
and Pista. I like the place. I have my own room with nice yellow
furniture with blue trim. Mother and Pista share the other bedroom. Mother is always busy. She drinks a lot of coffee and I am
not sure she hears me when I talk.

Pista doesn't look like my father. He is taller and very slim
and has blondish hair. He is very nice and I like him. He makes
me laugh a lot. He used to live in Vienna, Austria, until the Anschluss in 1938, when Germany took over Austria. He fled to
Hungary to avoid persecution as he was considered Jewish. He

had a printing company in Vienna and now he works in a print shop here in Budapest.

My school is all girls, twenty to a class. My teacher is Maria néni, and she is quite nice but very strict. She teaches us to read, write, count, and draw. Maria néni explains that she will be our teacher for our first four years of school and that it is quite important to do well with her and have good grades for high school. I also have Catholic religious instruction twice a week. Our teacher is a priest and he tells us the story about Adam and Eve and makes us repeat the Ten Commandments until we know them by heart.

At home we have a housekeeper during the day, Teresa, who picks me up from school, gives me lunch, and stays until Mother gets home from work. In the afternoon, after I finish my homework, Teresa takes me to the park, where I meet some of my friends from school. Most of them are there with their mothers. I wish my grandmother was there with me.

I do well in school and my teacher is pleased with my performance. I do not need tutoring in the summer. Since Mother and Pista are working, it is decided that I spend the summer with my cousins and Aunt Erzsi and Uncle Laci in Tápiógyörgye. They live on an estate, which Laci bácsi manages. They have an old farmhouse with chickens in the yard, two cows in the barn, and a horse-drawn buggy that they use to go everywhere. I like my cousins Tom and Marika. They are older than me but take me everywhere with them—swimming, bike riding, hiking. We have a good time.

In the fall, I go back to the city and stay with my grandparents again until school starts, and then I go back to live with Mother and Pista. In second grade, I am with the same children as in first grade, but school is harder. The hardest part is to learn the catechism by heart, which the priest expects us to do. He teaches us about the baby Jesus and his life and also about Jesus being crucified and killed by Jews. When I mention that at home, Mother doesn't take it too seriously. "You don't have to believe everything they say." But I do.

Our teacher Father Pal is really strict, preparing the class for first communion. Almost all of us in my class are going to have first communion, except a few girls who are Jewish and not converted like me, and the poor Presbyterians who have to go to their churches for religious education. I am very excited about the white dress I have to get for my communion. Mother is getting me a headband of white flowers, white shoes, white socks, and white gloves. I am doing well in my religion class. I am fascinated by the stories in the catechism, the Bible, and the sufferings of Jesus.

My first communion turns out to be a beautiful spring day. There is a party in the garden of the church to celebrate. I like what I am wearing. I see my father enter the garden and I think how handsome he is. He is tall with sparkling blue eyes and wavy black hair. Mother says to me, "You know he got married to Anni."

"Yes," I say. "I met her. She's nice."

"Anni néni is pretty," she says. "But it is your father who was always famous for his looks, yet it is his charm that gets you. He is always elegant—his suits look as though he was born in them. His mother, Kato néni, used to call him 'the Duke.'"

I spend the next summer with Kato néni at her house on the lake in Balatonlelle. In her younger years, Kato néni was a famous opera singer who played leading roles in major operas. Now retired, Kato néni still sings most of her conversations. She sings more than she speaks. The mailman, Miska, stops by every morning even if he has no mail to deliver to ask with a loud voice and a twinkle in his eyes, "Kato néni, my love, what would be your pleasure to sing for me today?"

She smiles, wags a finger at him, and sings. "Miska, Miska, you lazy boy. You would rather lean on the fence and listen to an old woman sing than carry your heavy bag and work. I shall have to speak to your mother about you, or maybe the post-master. But you are a growing boy still, and if you eat this nice piece of strudel I baked myself, I will have to forgive you, la la la la la. La la la la la."

There is laughter and applause from all around, from neighbors and passersby. They gather each day to watch the performance they have come to expect. When I first came to stay with Kato néni, her singing to friends and strangers embarrassed me, but soon enough, the songfests delight me. Often, I am the subject of her songs.

I was afraid that when I got back to Budapest, Mother was going to ask a lot of questions about my summer with Kato néni. I know I need to wipe the smile off my face so she is not upset that I enjoyed my visit with my grandmother. But Mother does not ask any questions. She looks funny. I find myself staring at her enlarged stomach. I'm not quite sure what it means. Pista notices my confusion and asks, "Do you like babies?" Before I have time to answer, Mother says, "You are going to have a little brother or sister."

She takes my hand and puts it on her stomach and lets me feel the baby's kick.

When Pista leaves the room, I ask Mother, "How does it get out?"

She points between her legs. "Yuck!" I think. I am really embarrassed.

* * *

YOM KIPPUR COMES AROUND in late fall and my grandparents spend the day in the synagogue fasting as observant Jewish people do. Mother wants to take me there to visit them. We do that every year but this time I don't want to go.

"Why not?" asks Mother.

"I will not set foot into a Jewish church," I answer. "It's a mortal sin."

"Mortal sin, shmortal sin," she says. "We are going."

"No," I shout. "No, I won't go!"

She lifts her hand to hit me, but I don't care. I don't want to be in mortal sin. She smacks me first, then grabs me and spanks me very hard. I am crying and wailing on the way to the synagogue. But I go.

Soon Mother stops working and my little sister, Katika, is born on December 14, 1942. When Mother brings the baby home, I can't believe she is real. She looks like a doll. But when the baby starts crying, it is real and loud. Mother teaches me how to change her diaper and wrap her up in swaddling clothes. I love the baby and can hardly wait to get home from school to be with her. By then, Mother is usually nicely dressed, and most of the time, weather permitting, we go to the park. Soon, I take over most of Katika's care, other than nursing, when I am home. She is my little sister but at times I feel like her mother.

CHAPTER TWO

BUDAPEST

· 1944 ·

MOTHER IS ON THE phone and I can hear that she is very upset. "No, no, no, it wasn't supposed to happen here." When she puts the phone down, she says, "Matyi's relatives have arrived." Matyi is the son of a German friend of my mother's. I am almost ten years old but I instantly know what that means. She is telling me, in code, that the Germans have invaded Hungary. Mother is worried that our building's superintendent, who is an informer for the Arrow Cross—the Hungarian Nazi Party—might be listening, as is his habit, and will report her as anti-German if he overhears our conversation. She sits down wringing her hands and crying, "From now on, it is going to get worse." The afternoon walk we were planning on this beautiful March day is canceled.

Soon, there are rumors about certain apartment houses being turned into collection stations for Jews before they are moved to the ghetto. They will be called "designated houses" and will be marked with a large yellow star painted on the main entrance. We don't know if our apartment house will be designated or not, but Mother doesn't want to take any chances. She starts to remove the valuable things in our apartment and distribute them for safekeeping with our Christian friends. Except for beds, tables, and other necessities, the apartment is almost empty but remains comfortable.

One day in April, when I come home from school, Mother is sitting at the table, the top of which is covered with yellow fabric. She is crying and muttering.

"What's the matter?" I ask her.

She doesn't answer.

I wonder what all of the yellow fabric is for. As I come closer, she turns to me and says with clenched teeth, "These will be the damn best yellow stars when I finish sewing."

A few minutes later, she turns to me again and explains, "As of tomorrow, anybody considered Jewish, even those who have converted, will have to wear a yellow star attached to their clothes: to a coat, a jacket, a dress—whatever they wear on the street. That is what I am making: yellow stars to wear."

She is telling me all of this but she is still crying. Her mascara is dripping. "Careful," I say, "you're staining the stars."

"I want to drown them," she says. "Now bring me your sweaters. We have to sew the stars on every coat and piece of clothing that you wear to school or outside."

I am not sure I understand. I'm thinking that I really don't want to wear the star. Why should I wear it? Maybe I can tear it off once I am out of the house. But it seems Mother reads my mind. "I'm going to accompany you to school tomorrow," she says. "I don't want you to walk alone wearing the star."

"I don't want to wear it," I say.

"You are not to even think about that. It is the law. As of today, not wearing the star if you are Jewish is a serious crime."

The next morning, Mother walks to school with me. Our

yellow stars announce from afar that we are Jewish. My school is only two and a half blocks away. As we walk down the second block, Mother begins to walk slowly, then she grabs my hand and starts to pull me across the street. "We are crossing here," she says. I'm not sure why and I don't want to go until I see Maria néni, my teacher, walking toward us. It's too late. She has seen us and she says, "Good day!" We stop and chat before we continue on our way.

"What a brave woman," Mother says. I don't understand why she says that until she tells me that if any Nazi or Arrow Cross informers had seen her chatting with us, they might report her for a crime called "sympathizing with the enemy."

We continue on our way to school and not a word is said about our yellow stars. When I walk into the classroom, I see that many of my classmates have yellow stars attached to their clothes too. I knew that some of my Catholic friends were Jewish but converted, like me. They too had their first communion, like me, and they do not consider themselves Jewish. Nor do I. Sunday Mass in the Basilica is important to them, just like it is to me. I feel embarrassed looking around but I know that they do too. We do not discuss our Jewish stars.

When our teacher, Maria néni, enters the class, there is silence until she says, "Good morning, all of you lovely girls." This is not her usual morning greeting. I feel better but still a sense of shame and embarrassment remains in the room. Classes go on as usual.

Soon, our apartment house is "designated" and wears a yellow star painted on its big brown entrance doorway. It frightens me every time I come home from school. The few Christian families who live in our building are instructed to move into other buildings. They leave gladly because they are allocated better, bigger, and nicer apartments that used to belong to Jews. The empty apartments in our building are filled with more Jewish families coming from non-designated houses. There are a lot more kids now and we are allowed to play on the covered porches at certain times of the day. But there are a lot of rules. You don't dare to offend the superintendent because he can get you deported.

I have been sharing a nanny with another girl whose mother is friends with my mother. We are supposed to learn German from her, because it is considered the second language of educated youth in Hungary. After school, we go to the park or walk around the city. Budapest is a very clean city with many wide avenues. There are stands selling frankfurters and roasted chestnuts. Sometimes we buy chestnuts. We converse in German as best we can while we walk, mostly in the inner city with its large apartment buildings, many shops, and coffeehouses on both sides of the Danube. We pass other designated houses on our walks. Sometimes we visit friends from school. All of the friends we visit live in designated houses. None of the other girls invite us anymore. Soon a curfew is ordered for Jews, and we have to stop our walks and our lessons.

Since the German takeover of the government, it has become illegal for Jews to own a radio. Everyone has to deliver theirs to specified authorities. Some days I am scared on my walk home from school when I see large printed papers plastered on the walls. They are mayoral decrees. Everyone is supposed to read them. These posts are the new rules for Jewish people. That's how we found out about the curfew. We are not allowed to go out more than two hours a day for shopping, walking, or going back and forth to school. We learned from these decrees that the penalty for a Jewish person not wearing a yellow star could be deportation or death. We are no longer allowed to go to the park.

Mother and Pista talk about these new rules a lot. I can tell how scared they are. There are many discussions about whom the decrees apply to. Mother's conversion to Catholicism did not save us from being considered Jews. Also, although Pista was born Catholic, he does not have four non-Jewish grandparents because his parents, who were originally Jewish, converted to Catholicism only before he was born. So Pista is Jewish.

Pista is of military age and one of the decrees states that converted Jewish men of military age have to register at a military center. He and Mother are talking about that decree.

"Do you realize that I will have to register tomorrow?" Pista says.

"You are Austrian," Mother replies. "Are they going to deport you back to Austria?"

"It is possible," he says.

"I think you will be better off if you find a way to stay here," Mother says, "even if it means going to a forced labor camp."

"I don't know if I will have a choice."

They are silent. I hear the words but I don't understand. I know they are afraid and I am too.

Pista registers but they don't tell him where he will have to go. He hopes that they will not call him soon. But one day when I come home from school, he is gone. Mother is crying and my Grandmother Adél is there crying too. Pista had to leave on a few hours' notice. We do not know where they have taken him, only that he is supposed to go to a forced labor camp on the front.

The next ordinances require that there be two people to a bedroom in designated houses. My Uncle Nandor moves in with us to prevent the government from putting strangers into my bedroom. Mother stays in her bedroom. Katika, sleeps in her pram in Mother's room. I don't actually share the bedroom with my uncle; I sleep in the hallway on a sofa. But Uncle Nandor does not stay with us too long. Mother sent him away because she did not like the way he looked at me. She tells the super that he went to visit his sister and will be back soon.

WE ARE GETTING A visitor. Mother is cleaning, although in this bare apartment there is not much to clean. Olga néni, who lives in a convent in Vienna, is coming. She is my stepfather, Pista's, mother and the grandmother of my little half-sister, Katika. Mother is excited. She is washing and ironing Katika's few pieces of clothing, making sure that the linens in the baby carriage are clean and neat. We keep the carriage in the apartment because we do not have a crib, but this is quite convenient as you can rock Katika to sleep right in her carriage and keep her happy without going for a walk. Mother does not like to take her for a walk in the few hours we are allowed to go out. She is afraid that some Arrow Cross soldier might kill her and Katika so he could take the pram back to his wife and their baby.

"Olga is coming," says Mother, "and we should be at our best. You know who she is?" she looks at me questioningly. "Or should I tell you again?"

"Yes," I say. I know that Olga néni is on her way to a small town called Bezdan in Yugoslavia to stay with her own mother and sister in the town they all came from. She is going to visit with us for a couple of days to get to know Katika, her only grandchild. I know this part of the story, but the rest of it is very confusing. I want to hear it again. I want to hear how Olga néni, my Jewish step-grandmother, became a nun.

"Simple," says my mother. "Just listen carefully."

She tells me the story of the young Olga and her husband, both from Bezdan, who were living in Vienna. He was a classical musician and she a translator of three different languages. Vienna was a very interesting city at that time, cultured but highly anti-Semitic. Olga and her husband decided to convert to Catholicism before they got married so that their children would be born Christian. Pista did not know about his Jewish origins until he was fourteen years old and his father died. After the death of her husband, Olga became more and more religious and eventually entered a convent and a few years later took her vows. She now belongs to a strict order. She is not allowed to leave the convent for visits. But her Mother Superior has given her permission to go to Bezdan to join her sick Jewish mother and her sister in the ghetto.

I understand the facts but I do not tell my mother how confused I am. Olga néni is a nun, but her son, my stepfather Pista, is in a forced labor camp as a Jew digging ditches on the Russian front. I am a Catholic because my mother converted us, but I have to wear a yellow star now when I go outside because I am considered Jewish. In school I go to Catholic religious class, but on Sunday when I have to go to Mass I have to have my yellow star showing on my coat. If I don't attend Mass, I get punished on Monday.

At Sunday Mass, there are lots of people—children and grown-ups—wearing yellow stars in the Basilica, the biggest Catholic church in the city. One Sunday, a fight starts after Mass in front of the church as we are leaving. People with yellow stars are spat at, called names, and beaten up. I hear a lot of ugly words—"you dirty Jew," "stealing our businesses," and similar insults. Suddenly, I feel a sharp pain on my shoulder. Somebody has hit me with a stick, and I fall. A lady helps me up and pulls me out of the melee, cursing the people who are causing the trouble. "They are all out of their minds," she says. "They are agitators. Are you all right? Where do you live?" My grandparents live close to the Basilica, and that's the address I give her. She takes me to their apartment and advises my grandmother to call our doctor—it is obvious that I have been hurt. As it turns out, I have a broken shoulder bone that remains painful for a long, long time. I wish I didn't have to go back to church with a yellow star.

Olga néni arrives in the afternoon. I love the way she looks in her flowing black habit with just two starched white pieces of cloth sticking out about where her ears must be. She looks a bit like Mickey Mouse. She does not have a stern face. She is smiling a lot and asks me questions about everything—my school, my friends, my religious education—but Mother interrupts that subject with an offer of some tea. Katika is friendly and bubbly as if she knew to be on her best behavior. As it turns out, Olga néni wants to leave the next day. Her sick mother is getting worse and she wants to get to her as soon as possible. We go to sleep early. Olga néni sleeps in Mother's room and takes off only her shoes and the veil on her head. Mother sleeps with me on my sofa, and Katika sleeps in her pram.

There is an air raid in the middle of the night. Mother says it's going to be a bad one judging by the intensity and frequency of the sirens. Olga néni doesn't want to go to the air raid shelter in the basement with us, but Mother insists. When we come into the shelter, everybody stops talking and they are all looking at us. Actually, they are all looking at Olga néni in her habit. She stands out against the rest of us in dressing gowns and sloppy clothing. Soon the conversation starts again, but it is subdued as if the unexpected presence of a nun has intimidated everybody. A man from the fourth floor moves closer, inching his way toward Olga néni. "Oh, my dear," he says, reaching for her habit. "What wonderful fabric. Peace-time quality. Where did you get it? It is amazing how the good quality makes your disguise look so authentic. You must have paid a lot of money for this."

I look around and notice that Mother is embarrassed by his behavior. I wish he would stop, but he continues, ignoring the spreading silence as more and more people stop talking and pay curious attention to see what's going to happen. Then the man from the fourth floor asks, "When are you trying to make your escape? I guess you'll leave in the daylight. Nuns don't go out at night. Have you arranged for a convent to accept you?" He is very excited. He doesn't seem to realize that his questions are not being answered. When he finally stops, Olga néni raises both of her hands and smiles at everybody.

Then she says in a gentle and clear voice, "This habit is truly authentic. It took me seven years of hard work and a lot of prayer until I could make my vows and become a nun in spite of my Jewish origins. If I knew where you could get one as a disguise, I would certainly let you know, especially if there was a chance that it might help you to get away from persecution. I am on the way to join my mother and my sister in the Bezdan ghetto. I wish you all the best and will include you in my prayers."

After that, people are silent until we hear the sirens signaling the end of the air raid.

"Stop . . . stop . . . stop," Mother hisses at me. I am sitting on a pillow Mother put on the bare floor, pretending to be cooking my favorite foods in some pots and pans. It is going to be a delicious meal. It will look and taste just like the meals my grandmother Kato néni used to cook for me. In reality, we eat enough bread, potatoes, and cabbage to keep me from being very hungry, but we can't get the ingredients for the foods I really like. Many stores are not willing to sell to Jews wearing the yellow star, and buying on the black market, my mother says, is too expensive and very dangerous. I am surprised that I have to stop playing. Usually, she likes me to play kitchen, but now she wants me to be quiet as she anxiously peers out the window. Turning back to me, she says one word. "Razzia!"

It means "checking on the Jews" in the designated houses. It is carried out by members of the Arrow Cross.

I am not yet ten years old, but I can see how nervous my mother is. Pacing up and down and thinking out loud, she says, "It is a raid, but we are on the third floor. It will take them a while to get up here depending on whether they find anything to steal or anybody to deport on the way up. It will be at least twenty minutes before they get to us."

I do not understand why she is so scared, as she has often said, "Everything is completely legal." We don't have anything worth stealing in this apartment anymore. The floors are bare. Our Persian rugs and most of our furniture have been put in safe keeping with some Christian friends. We no longer have any paintings that are valuable. My room still has some furniture in it, a bed and a table, but nothing else.

Now she turns to me and she says in her most serious voice, "I know you are a responsible girl. Here is what I want you to do. When the soldiers bang on the door, you open it. When they ask where your mother is, tell them sweetly that she is taking a bath, and ask them if they want you to call her. Just stand there and wait to hear what the soldiers say. If they want to come in, let them. If they want to wait in the living room, let them. Don't do anything that could make them think that you are lying. Tell them again I am in the bath, and I will be. If they come in, they will hear the water running."

"Didn't you have a bath this morning?" I ask. Our hot water supply is not very good and it is very expensive. We have to be careful how much hot water we use. It is heated by a gas burner on a small tank on the wall, and after we ignite it, it takes a long time until the water gets hot. If you want to have a really hot bath, you have to leave the burner going all the time. Our cold water, on the other hand, comes from an old tap on the wall, and it is very noisy.

We hear some commotion outside. She says, "Quickly. I'll explain. We don't have much time. It is not I who is taking a bath. I didn't want you to know, but now I have to tell you. I won't be in the tub. I need some time to melt the two pounds of sugar I bought on the black market yesterday." We are not allowed to have any sugar beyond the meager portions we receive with our ration card. She says, "If they find the sugar, they'll take us away. They will kill both of us and throw us in the Danube. Or they'll send us to a concentration camp."

When the soldiers carry out their raids, they look for things Jews are not allowed to have: radios, cigarettes, certain foods like chocolate, sugar, and anything else that may catch their fancy. Lately, the German SS themselves are carrying out some of the raids. During the last one in our building, the old couple living on our floor on the other side of the elevator disappeared. They were never seen again. Nobody speaks of what they had that the soldiers wanted.

Mother disappears into the bathroom. I can hear the water

running. I am really scared. My legs are shaking. Soon, there is a knock on our door. I open it. Two German soldiers are standing there. One asks, "Mother?" I can tell he doesn't speak much Hungarian. I don't even say, "Bath." I just motion them in and point. "Bathroom," I say. The soldiers are near the bathroom door now, and they can hear the water running. "Is the door locked?" one of them asks in broken Hungarian.

I try to think quickly. If I say yes, they might rattle the door; if I say no, they might open it. I say, "Locked?" in a shocked voice. "Oh no, my mother would never lock me out." The soldiers lose interest and walk into the living room. They see the pram and ask, "Baby?" I say, "Grandmother." They lift the cover on the pram and see that Katika is not there. Mother took her to my grandparents' house this morning. (She usually does that when she goes to work, but today she came back after she dropped off Katika because I had no school this morning.) The soldiers, looking out the bare window to the street below, seem bored. They take another look around and leave.

"Mother, come out of the bathroom," I call and I open the door. She is still trying to flush the last bits of a paper bag that held the sugar down the toilet. She has torn the bag into little pieces, but it takes a while. They wouldn't all flush at once. If the soldiers had opened the door, they would have found her in all of her clothes, the water running, and pieces of the paper bag floating in the toilet. All the sugar is gone. Mother turns off the water, but she is crying and I don't know if she is crying because she is still afraid. Or is she happy? But then she looks at me and says, "We are never going to have two pounds of sugar again."

CHAPTER THREE

BUDAPEST TO KISLÁNG

· Spring 1944 ·

I AM EXCITED BECAUSE my father, Henry, is coming to visit. I have seen him only once since our house became designated and the big yellow star was placed on the front door. Before, he used to pick me up every Sunday, but now, since he does not have to wear a yellow star, it is dangerous for him to visit a designated house and even more so to take a kid out who is wearing a yellow star. "Why is he coming today?" I ask Mother. "And anyway, how come he is not wearing a yellow star? Is he not Jewish like we are? Or is it the divorce?"

"Oh, no," she says. She looks exasperated, and I expect her to tell me to stop asking so many questions. But she does not. Instead, she tells me to sit down and she will explain again. She tried to make me understand once before, but I still do not get it. I know I am Jewish, and I know I am also a Catholic. So what is my father? Neither? How come? "Maybe he is not my father?" I asked Mother some time ago and she really got mad at me. She called me a stupid girl who talks too much, and I started to cry. "Your father is your father," she had said. "Now, stop crying and stop behaving like a child."

Now she wants me to listen very carefully. I can tell it is important. "First of all," she begins her explanation, "the question of why he is exempt by law from being Jewish has nothing to do with our divorce, but a lot to do with his marriage to Anni. You know Anni and I think you like her. She is a good-hearted, pretty woman, and she is not now and never has been Jewish. The government has recently forbidden Jews to marry Christians, but if they were *half*-Jews converted and already married to a Christian when this law was passed, they could stay married and be considered Christian." She stops. "Do you understand me so far?"

"Yes, I do," I say. "My father is half-Jewish because his mother, my grandmother Kato néni, is Jewish, but her first husband, my grandfather, is not. So my father can be a Christian because of his marriage to Anni. I still want to know why Father can't pick me up on Sundays to go to my grandmother's for the delicious lunches she always cooks for me."

Mother explains to me that my grandmother is living in a designated house and is just as restricted as we are in who can visit her and what foods she can get. It has become dangerous for my father to visit his mother or us. He is taking a chance coming to see us.

"So why," I ask, "is he coming to see us? It is not even Sunday."

I think Mother is smiling as she continues, but what she explains next is very serious and scares me. She makes me understand that designated houses are collection places from where Jews are taken to the ghetto or concentration camps. My father is trying to save us from being forced to go to a ghetto. He has a way to smuggle us out of this building and get us to a small village in eastern Hungary, where we will live as non-Jews who do not have to wear a yellow star.

"So how come we won't have to wear the yellow star?" I ask. "It is the law? How is Father going to do that?"

"I will tell you," Mother says. "I will explain to you how we will escape. Your father is bringing us a whole set of fake documents, birth certificates, for you, me, and Katika, a passport for me with my childrens' names in it, information on fake grandparents, and some other documents we might need. Both you and I have to learn our new identities, names, and our history, where we used to live, the school you supposedly attended, names of your friends, your teachers, and of course, the name of your *fake* father. We will have to do this in a short period of time. We cannot take the chance of another raid when they might find all the papers. Or worse, we might already have been moved to the ghetto."

There is knock on the door. My father is here. I am so happy to see him. He walks in and lifts me up to kiss and hug me. I am almost ten years old and I am not used to being treated like a little kid but I don't mind it. I love the words he uses. "You are a beautiful young lady," he says. "You are my star, my angel, my pride."

Mother interrupts, sternly, "Enough of that!"

They sit down at the table and talk in very low voices. They must think that I do not hear them, but I do. Father is explaining the route we will take in a few days to the railway station. He gives her the tickets and many other papers and starts to discuss our invented family. I no longer pay attention and play with Katika until I hear my name.

"Do you think," asks Father, "that Erika will be able to learn all about her new name, identity, and the history of the fake family in time?"

"Or course," says Mother. "She is my daughter, isn't she?"

There is some discussion about luggage. We mustn't take any with us. "I know a Jewish woman from another designated house," Father says, "who will collect some of your things tomorrow— not too much. She will have to make two trips because she will not want to draw suspicion with too many packages. No suit- cases." He is looking at my mother. "Don't worry. I have ar- ranged for Katika's baby needs, even a crib, which is all waiting for you in Kisláng."

He gets up to leave and says to me, "Just make sure you don't share any of this information with anyone. Nobody, nobody can know about this." I hear what he says and realize how serious this is. I'm afraid.

Father looks at my mother—lovingly, I think. "I know it will be difficult," he says, "but I'm not worried about you. I trust you. You can do this."

Mother looks up at him and I wonder why she doesn't say anything, but then I see tears running down her face. Father looks sad. He plants a big kiss on my forehead and he leaves.

Mother sits at the table motionless. I have so many questions but dare not interrupt her silence. Katika is restless. I change her diaper and bring her to mother to nurse. Mother has not moved. I am hungry too.

"What will we have for dinner?" I ask. She instructs me to take the cabbage soup out of the icebox and to heat it up for dinner. I don't know why we keep it in the icebox; there is no ice in the box. We no longer go downstairs in the morning when the iceman calls. Mother thinks it is dangerous to go out on the street. So we have no ice. We don't have much food to keep in the icebox anyway. Right now, there is the cabbage soup she cooked two days ago, some bread, a tiny piece of butter she bought this morning, and two precious eggs. We don't buy any milk as Mother is breastfeeding and she likes her coffee black. We have a small piece of cheese that sits on the kitchen table. Cheese is not supposed to be refrigerated anyhow.

After we eat the soup and some bread, Mother starts to teach me my new identity. My first name stays the same. My new family name is Bankuti. My fake father is a soldier on the Russian front, and he is a much-decorated officer. We continue learning until I can no longer keep my eyes open. The next morning, we do the same. Mother decides to keep me at home and calls my school to tell them that I am sick. She uses the telephone in the janitor's office downstairs. As he is employed by the government, he happily reports any irregularities the Jews may commit. But he gladly takes ten forints from any Jew who wants to use his telephone.

The lessons are very hard. I have a good memory, but there is so much to remember and not much time to do it. I think maybe we will leave in a few days, but Mother will not tell me when. "You cannot give up what you do not know," she says. I know it is soon, because she is not letting me go back to school. We spend the next few days rehearsing our new identities.

One night she wakes me up and asks me my name.

"Erika Bleier," I say.

"What did you say?" she asks. Her voice is dangerous. "Erika Bleier," I repeat fearfully, realizing too late that I made a mistake. Even to her I was supposed to lie and use my fake name, Erika Bankuti. Her anger boils over. She hits me with her open palm across my face and hisses through clenched teeth, "If you ever make that mistake again, we will be killed!"

I never utter that name again.

• • •

THE NEXT MORNING, MOTHER puts two suits on, wearing two sweaters and a shirt under the jackets. It is April and not that cold, so I think today is the day. She puts an extra cardigan out for me and tells me to be careful. "Careful of what?" I ask.

"Your yellow star," she says. "It is very loosely attached, and I don't want you to lose it before we are ready to take it off completely. Mine is loose too, but we will take them off only when I tell you."

"Where are we going?" I ask. But she is not willing to tell me.

"Listen to me as we go along, and do as I say."

We leave as if for a walk. We go away from the city center toward buildings that are mostly used for government offices. What is my mother doing? I think it is very dangerous to be in this area. There are many guards, soldiers, and police. As we turn a corner, my mother says, "Take off your sweater and fold it over your arm so that the star doesn't show." Then she moves Katika, whom she has been carrying, from one side of her chest to the other. And I realize that the way she is now holding my sister covers her own star. Next, we walk into a large municipal building. She smiles at the guard at the door and says, "We have an appointment with Mr. Szabo on the fourth floor."

The guard is very polite and directs us to the elevator. We take it to the second floor, and we turn right when we get off. I don't dare to ask why we got off here. Two doors from the elevator there is a toilet with a little anteroom. We go inside, and I open my mouth to ask her my questions, but she shushes me and checks out the two stalls. Neither of them is occupied. She hands me Katika. With one swift motion, she tears off the star from her suit and crumples it up in her hand, then takes my

DON'T ASK MY NAME

sweater and disappears into one of the stalls. She flushes the toilet several times and comes out just as a lady enters the bathroom. She smiles brightly at the lady while she hands me my sweater and takes Katika from me. We leave. I am surprised when we do not turn left to take the elevator, but turn right and walk past a guard, walk down the stairs, and exit through another door. As we are walking away, I say, "How did you know what to do? How did you do this?" She promises to tell me later, but now we must hurry to the station to take the train to our hiding place. Then she adds, "You can thank your father the next time you see him."

We are walking very fast toward the railroad station. I can barely keep up and I say, "Can we slow down a bit?"

"We must not miss the train," says Mother.

Close to the station, she does slow down. "We don't want to look harassed or nervous," she says. "The Army is controlling the station, and we don't want to be noticed when we get there." She tells me that she knows which platform our train will leave from because my father explained it all to her.

We find the platform and are walking alongside the train looking at the numbers of the box cars to find the one that matches our tickets when I see Jani.

"Jani," I yell.

He's inside the train, looking out of the open window of a compartment. He sticks his arm out and points to the door where we are supposed to enter. I love Jani. I have known him all my life. He is the manservant my father shares with his brother and started working for them on Father's eighteenth birthday. Most young men from good families are expected to have manservants, but few keep them beyond a couple of years. Jani is still working part-time for the family and is trusted and loved by all.

He comes from a large peasant family from rural Hungary. He has never mentioned the village's name, only that it was "godforsaken." Jani loves my father and is totally loyal to us.

It's good to see him here, waving and smiling. But why is he in the compartment we have tickets for, and how come I see some luggage and some food, too? Jani has been busy making sure we are comfortable. He adjusts the blanket that he puts on two of the seats so that Katika can lie down. He pours Mother some coffee from a thermos and puts it on the little table between two facing seats next to the window. I wonder why Mother doesn't seem to be surprised to see him. She busies herself with Katika and lets Jani answer all of my questions.

I haven't seen him for a long time. He had not come to visit since before our house became a designated house. I am so excited talking to him. "Jani," I ask, "where are we going?"

"You are going to my village, Kisláng," he says.

"Is that where you come from? Is that where your family lives?"

"Yes," he says. Then he tells me about his parents, his four brothers, their wives and kids, and one sister with her brood. Jani's other sister, who is older, married into another village and does not come to visit very often. "We are seven and I am the youngest and the only one who got away to the city."

Mother interrupts, "What time exactly does this train leave?"

"Not yet," answers Jani. "We have about ten minutes if the train is on time."

"Are you coming with us?" I ask.

"Yes," he says, "but I will be sitting in the back in the caboose with the other housemen on this train. When we arrive, I will help you off the train and introduce you to my uncle. He will be waiting for you with his horse-drawn wagon and will take you to

Kisláng, which is about twenty kilometers away. He is my mother's brother, and everybody in the village calls him Varga bácsi."

"What about you, Jani? Aren't you coming with us too?" I ask.

"No," says Jani. "My father will be waiting to take me for a quick visit to my mother."

"Jani," I say, "you won't be staying with us?"

"No," he says again, "I am returning to Budapest on the evening train. I have to be back tonight." He turns to my mother and says, "Mrs. Bankuti."

I look around to see what Mrs. Bankuti, a lady with such a good old Hungarian name, is doing in our compartment, before I realize that he is talking to my mother.

"I told the conductor that he has some important travelers today, seeing that your husband is a high-ranking officer in the Army and that he is on the front. I think you will find him most polite. Besides," he adds, "the journey is only about four or five hours."

I am glad that he said "Bankuti" because seeing him and feeling more comfortable made me almost forget that we were traveling under a false identity. It is a reminder that I have to use my new name if anybody asks. As if he knew what I was thinking, Jani turns to me and says, "Remember, your name is Bankuti, Erika. And remember, too, that from the time you arrive in Kisláng, you do not know me nor have you met anybody in my family. If you make a mistake, it could be dangerous for me too."

I want to ask him so many more questions but it's time for him to go. The train will leave in a few minutes, and he must get to the caboose. He smiles and makes a little bow in the direction of my mother. "Madame Bankuti and the two Bankuti girls," he says, "have a safe journey." He leaves, closing the compartment door behind him.

Mother sinks into a seat with a deep sigh. Finally, she says, "I am so glad that five extra tickets were provided so that we can have the whole compartment to ourselves." She does not mention that it was my father who bought the tickets. It seems to me that for the sake of our safety, he must now be forgotten.

I do start to understand. From now on, we really have to be these other people, "the Bankutis," who are Christian, aristocratic, and rich enough to buy eight tickets for only one adult and two children.

When the conductor knocks on the door and looks through the glass, I get scared. He wears a dark uniform with gold buttons, and I think for a minute that he is a policeman who has come to arrest us and take us off the train. But Mother is smiling and reaches into her bag for our tickets, which the conductor takes. He looks at them only briefly. She reaches into her purse again and pulls out a large bill. She gives it to him when he hands the tickets back and says, "I know that there are several stops before we reach Kisláng. If more people get on the train, please stop them from trying to get into this compartment."

The conductor smiles and says, "Thank you, madam, I will make sure you are not disturbed." Mother seems satisfied with the promise. Soon, I hear the hissing of the steam engine and then the noise of the wheels starting to turn, first a slow tack-tack and then, as they go faster and faster, a-tack, a-tack, a-tack, a-tack until I look out the window and see the station and the city behind us.

In the compartment, Mother's eyes are closed. I am very hungry now and very tired as well. Katika is asleep. Mother fed her when we first got on the train. Now it's my turn to eat. As Mother opens her eyes, she reaches for the bag with the sandwiches that Jani left behind. He knows us well enough to have provided all the delicious things we like, and he remembered to pack one of my favorites—a large crunchy water roll spread with goose fat and slices of goose liver. For dessert, there is some fruit and cherries, the first of the season, as well as cookies. The cookies, too, are my favorites, little crunchy round-shaped sugary biscuits with a drop of jam in the middle. After my lunch, I watch the landscape speed by, and then I fall asleep.

Mother wakes me, telling me we will be in Kisláng in about five minutes. She has already gotten Katika ready, and the "friendly" conductor has come to take the luggage off the shelves. The luggage is all new; I have never seen it before. The bags must have been bought by my father and put on the train by Jani. I am sure that they are full of clothes for mother, Katika, and me.

When the train finally comes to a stop, Jani is there to help us. When we get out and step on the ground, I see that everything is dust and I start worrying about my shoes. But there is no time for that now, says Mother. We are introduced to Jani's uncle, Varga bácsi. He is not a young man. Varga bácsi looks like what I imagine peasants look like, with a dark vest and floating shirt and pants, the customary clothing of the area. He smiles and lifts me into the wagon. Jani says goodbye and I can tell he is almost crying. I am afraid I will cry too. I look away and get busy watching several horse-drawn carriages at the station, some chickens in the field next to the train tracks, and a boy about my age dressed in short pants and a shirt that is not tucked in. He looks different from my friends in the city. I haven't been to the country since I stayed a few years ago with my Aunt Erzsi and Uncle Laci and my cousins Tom and Marika. I liked staying with them when I was six years old, so I am very excited to look around now and imagine telling them about being in the country again. Suddenly, I remember that I do not have cousins called

Tom or Marika. According to my new identity, all my cousins are Bankutis and they live in Budapest or in northern Hungary. I am supposed to have stayed with them every summer.

So there are no cousins Tom and Marika, nobody to talk to about what I am really thinking, because I must not give us away. I must not. Maybe the best way I can do that is not to speak at all. I decide to talk as little as possible.

We arrive in the village and stop in front of a little house that has a gate and a tiny front garden. A path leads to the door. Varga bácsi takes our luggage and puts it down in the middle of the room, which turns out to be the kitchen, living room, and Katika's bedroom. Mother's bedroom is to the right and is very small. I will sleep with her

"If you need anything or if you are missing anything," Varga bácsi says, "tell me the next time when I come to see you. But I think you'll find everything in order." He shows us the wood stacked in the corner and explains how to light the fire in the hearth in the kitchen and the stove next to it. "The fresh milk in the covered pot is from this morning and so is the bread and butter," he continues. "And the water in the sink should not be rusty. I let it run a lot yesterday. So, I wish you a good day. Take a rest, and I will see you later."

I want to use the toilet and we go looking for it. There is one attached to the house, behind the porch with the entrance from the outside, but it is a real toilet with a tank hanging on the top of the wall and a pull on a long chain. There is only one sink in the house, the one that is in the kitchen, so that probably will be our washroom. "This sink is barely big enough to put Katika in it," says Mother. "And you and I will have to use the basin as well. It's not very large, but at least we don't have to boil too much water to fill it."

Mother sinks down on the bench near the fireplace and says, "We'll unpack and find room for everything later. Right now, I want to explain to you how we got to Kisláng and why we are here. You know some of this already. But let me repeat it to you because I don't want you to make any mistakes. A mistake, even a small one, could mean deportation and death for all of us. Well, you know about our false name and our fake papers and invented history. I'd like you to repeat all of it to yourself several times a day so that you cannot be caught unaware if anybody asks you a question. Jani, on the other hand, should never be mentioned." She explains that some villagers might know that he was working for a Jew in the city. "In my eyes," says Mother, "he's a hero because he is the one who offered to your father to bring us to safety here in his village with the cooperation of his whole family."

Then she warns me that I might have a big surprise when I go out. She tells me that my father also arranged for his mother, his sister (my Aunt Hedi), and my cousins Jutka and Zsuzsa to stay in this village with Varga bácsi and his family. My Uncle Richard's wife, Manyi, and my cousin Robert are also hidden in another part of the village, staying with another relative of Jani's. The village is mostly run by Varga bácsi and his and Jani's relatives, so it is possible to arrange hiding places for all of us. "Of course," says Mother, "it is very important that none of us makes a mistake about our assumed identities. As I said to you before, it could be deadly for us and for Jani and his relatives too."

She continues, "You have to remember that you do not know them. You cannot visit them. You cannot say hello to your cousins. We probably will be introduced to each other in a day or two, according to Varga bácsi, so that we do not have to act like strangers. You must always remember, though, that your name is Bankuti."

I am surprised to learn that my grandmother Kato néni and all of my father's family are staying safely here too. I ask, "How was all of this arranged?"

"I think Jani offered your father houses in the village that were available for rent. Your father arranged it all. Of course," she continues, "I am referring to your real father, not your fake hero father on the front. What is his name again?"

I am blank for only a second, and then it comes to me: "Bankuti, Jozsef."

We are silent for a moment, and then we look at each other and smile. I realize that it is the first time I came out with an answer that is a lie but nevertheless correct.

CHAPTER FOUR

KISLÁNG

• Summer 1944 •

I LIKE IT IN Kisláng. At first it is strange: no school, no grandparents, no yellow star on my clothes. Mother is not quite as short-tempered as she was in Budapest, nor does she whisper about the danger we are in and how to behave to avoid it. She is busy, cleaning the little house, doing the laundry in the iron sink that stands on legs under a rickety cold-water tap. We heat the water on the stove for everything, not just the laundry but for washing ourselves, bathing Katika, and for cooking, of course. We do quite a lot of cooking. Varga bácsi brings us potatoes, meat, milk, and some fruit, too, mostly apples. We do not leave the house very much, as Mother decided that I better not meet my cousins or my grandmother at all, for fear somebody somehow would find out that we knew each other before we came to Kisláng. Varga bácsi agrees that this is best. "It is safer to be separate, unrelated families," he says, "who have come from the big city to escape the bombings and the lack of food."

Mother is still nursing Katika, but my sister now eats people food, too. I often take her for a little walk, play with her, and teach her to talk. Every time I push the stroller through the gate to take Katika for a walk, Mother is nervous. She says to me, "Don't you make a big mistake and say hello if you happen to see your grandmother." She repeats that every time I leave. I don't go very far. The sidewalk is just a narrow strip of earth between the houses and the ditch. The main road is also a dirt road, and usually muddy with deep grooves from the horse-drawn wagons—the only traffic you ever see in this village. It is difficult to cross the street. There are small strips of earth filling the ditches here and there, but they are too narrow for the stroller. Katika is sixteen months old and does not really walk yet. "Katika," I say to her, "see the chickens. Let's try to catch one." Or, "Look at the geese." There are beautiful white geese running around on the road. I wonder how they know which house they belong to or how their owners know which chicken or goose belongs to them when it is time for them to go home.

I cross the road carrying Katika and leave the stroller on the side of the street near our house. I am going to visit Laci bácsi and Sara néni, who live across the street from us with their children, twelve-year-old Marta and ten-year-old Janos. They are both teachers at the local school, the only two teachers in the village. The village, small as it is, provides each of its teachers with a house. Laci bácsi and Sara néni are married, so they live in one of their houses, the bigger one, and we are staying in the other. I like to visit with them. They are nice and they show me interesting books and photographs around their house, and often we stay in the garden. It's like having lessons in geography, botany, and biology.

Some of the geese they own are ready to be prepared for the market. Sara néni explains, "They have to be fattened up before they are sold, to develop the large fatty livers that are the basis of the famous Hungarian goose liver."

"Better than the French," Laci bácsi is fond of saying.

I am taught a lesson on how to force-feed the geese. We go to the chicken coop, which also houses the cages that the geese live in, while Marta and Janos play with Katika.

"The geese must not run around or even walk," Laci bácsi explains, "or they will not gain enough weight to fetch a good price at the market."

I am sitting on the stool in the geese's corner, holding a beautiful white bird tightly between my knees. "The beak has to face out," warns Laci bácsi, "so that you will not be nipped. They are not the best-natured animals. The next step is tricky." He shows me how to force the goose's mouth open in order to push handfuls of dried corn into it. "You have to press on both sides of his beak and not let go, until you have put the corn into the open mouth of the animal. Next you have to close his mouth by pressing the beak together or he will spit it out."

I follow his instructions and wonder what is next. "Hold the beak tightly together with your left hand," he says, "and place your right hand on his neck and start stroking it, gently up and down at first and stronger as you go along."

I do as I am told and notice that soon the goose starts to swallow. "Help him a little more," says the teacher. "All the food from his mouth has to go to his stomach."

Pushing stronger and faster all the time, I feel the corn passing into the goose's stomach. But I am more and more uncomfortable doing this. I pity the goose and I am reminded of how my mother back in Budapest long ago tried to force me to eat some thick green soup that I found very distasteful, pushing a spoonful of it through my closed mouth.

"It is so good for you, full of vitamins," she had said. "We hardly ever eat vegetables anymore, and when we do get them, they are so very expensive. You have to eat it."

"I don't care," I had said, but talking was a mistake. She quickly forced another spoonful into my open mouth. But this time I could not swallow it. I retched, and all of the food she had forced into me came back, landing mostly on her. She hit my face with an open palm and warned, "Next time you will not get anything else to eat until you finish your vegetables."

Laci bácsi teaches me much more about the food we eat. They have a big field behind their house with lots of growing things—corn on one side on a long strip of land, then grains behind that. He explains how these things wind up being food. I find that very interesting. I want to know more about it and look forward to more lessons. I particularly enjoy their vegetable garden. It is big and fenced in, and a lot of the food that I like grows there. When you want to eat something, you just pull it out of the earth: radishes, potatoes, carrots. I see the green peppers ripening on bushes and peas and green beans on stalks. I am surprised because I did not know how these things grew before we came to Kisláng. Sometimes Laci bácsi takes me to their barn and lets me watch him milk the cows. They have two of them called Mu and Mo. He pats them on their behind and praises them after he milks them. "They are very good milk givers," he says. He loves all his animals, except one of their two horses who does not listen to him when harnessed to the buggy. The horse follows only Sara's instructions and that annoys Laci bácsi, but he smiles and I understand that he is not angry at the horse at all.

Often when Laci bácsi is teaching me about the countryside, Katika stays in the yard or inside the house with the children or with Sara néni. School is over and they are all at home, but they are always busy, in the fields or in the gardens or with the animals. My favorite activity is collecting eggs. They have a lot of chickens and a lot of eggs have to be picked up every day.

•   •   •

FATHER VISITS EVERY SATURDAY. He takes the train from Budapest to a station near Kisláng. I sit with Varga básci on the front bench of the buggy when we go to pick up my father. Varga básci even lets me hold the reins sometimes and tells me stories about his horse misbehaving, wanting to go right when he wants him to go straight, or spitting on his friend when he stops the buggy for a little chat with him. I am excited when I see Father get off the train. He is smiling at me and waving even before he reaches us. Father is carrying a small suitcase and climbs on the buggy, sitting down next to me on the bench. I must remember not to be too friendly, as he is not supposed to be my father, although I don't see anybody at the station who might recognize us. When I say that to Varga bácsi, he says, "Being careful has never hurt anyone." I try not to jump all over Father and sit quietly between him and Varga bácsi on the bench.

I know why he is here and I know what comes next. He opens the little suitcase that he is holding on his lap and takes out a package. It is cigarettes for Mother. Next, he lifts the newspaper that covers the rest of what is in the suitcase and shows the contents to Varga bácsi. The first time I saw that the suitcase was full of money, I was surprised. Mother explained to me later that Father was paying for all of our expenses, including the upkeep of his own mother, his sister, his sister-in-law, and all the cousins, all of them staying with relatives of Varga bácsi. "It seems to me that as long as your father brings the money every week, we are all safe."

Back at the little house, we have dinner together, Father explaining how the war is going. "The Russians," he says, "are fast progressing, pushing back the Germans from Russian territory.

They have now entered eastern Hungary, and it seems logical that they will reach the Austrian border before the Americans or the British can get there. Although the Allied Forces are making great gains in the West, it is clear that if Hungary is to be liberated, it will be by the Russians."

He tells my mother, "In Budapest, I have a contact who informs me how family and friends are adjusting to the ghetto. Your parents are doing pretty well and receive extra food regularly through my contacts. On the other hand," he continues, putting his arm around Mother's shoulder, "I'm sorry but I have no news of Pista from the forced labor camp on the Russian front."

After Katika is asleep, I am instructed to take my pillow and blanket from Mother's bed, where I usually sleep, and place it on the bench between Katika's carriage and the stove in the kitchen. I don't know what upsets me more—giving up my nice comfortable place next to Mother in the bed, or the vague realization that it is not right for my father to sleep with my mother who is now the wife of another man.

Breakfast turns out to be happy for them. The early fall weather is beautiful. Father is sitting outside at a little table in his underwear, and Mother in her slip serves him breakfast. I overhear Father telling her that he loves her dark eyes and her girlish body. "Your legs are perfect," he says. Mother is smiling blissfully and listening as Father hums a song to her. They look as if they are in love. If that's the way they feel about each other, why did they divorce? Why do I not have my father living with us? I'm getting confused. It's not fair. As I watch them, I'm getting sick to my stomach. I walk away to throw up in the bushes. Then I go inside to tend to Katika.

Soon, though, Father no longer visits. It has become too

dangerous to travel so close to the front lines to make the trip from Budapest to Kisláng. He arranges weekly payments to Varga bácsi through Jani, so that our safe haven in the village is not threatened.

When Mother runs out of cigarettes, she takes out tobacco leaves that Father had brought her, and which she keeps hidden in a big bag under the bed. She wants me to cut the tobacco fine enough to roll it into cigarettes. I have to wet the leaves first, just a little, so I can roll them up tightly without breaking them, and then slice them as finely as possible. They are then ready to be dried and rolled. When she runs out of rolling paper, she uses newspaper. I think it looks terrible and it frightens me to see a thick roll of burning newspaper hanging out of her mouth. But then she tells me how well I cut the tobacco, so very, very thin, and I keep on cutting it for her when she asks me to.

It is early September and school is starting. I am not allowed to go. I think Mother, Laci bácsi, and Sara néni decided that it is better to give me lessons at their home. "Those kids in class would tease you for being from the city," Mother says. She further explains that she thinks the kids will ask me questions, like how many cousins I have, or how many aunts and uncles, and many other questions to satisfy their curiosity. Therefore, she has arranged with Laci bácsi and Sara néni to give me private lessons, so that I should not fall too far behind in my studies. "But anyway," she says, "many schools closer to the front lines are not going to open, and the ones farther east, already under Russian occupation, are closed."

We have a big radio. It gets only Hungarian and German stations. All other signals are blocked. We get some news about the progress of the war. Mother gets angry when she listens and sometimes talks back to the radio. "Idiots, morons!" she yells, using some other words I am not supposed know. "The problem," says Mother, "is that they don't tell the truth. Every time the German/Hungarian Army retreats, it is announced as a 'victory' or a 'planned retreat.'"

We have another radio we keep hidden. Father brought it to us earlier in the summer. It is a small and heavy shortwave radio and has a long antenna that folds and can be moved in search of reception. If it is positioned right, you can listen to many forbidden foreign stations: French, English, and other languages, which we do not understand. It is very dangerous to listen to as it is strictly forbidden by the government. There is one broadcast we manage to catch late at night. It is the BBC News Hungarian edition. It is jammed but some of the signal gets through. It crackles and whistles and you can barely hear it, but we manage to get an idea of where the front lines really are and that the Germans are in fact retreating more and more. The Russians are fast approaching, and Mother predicts that they will reach us by Christmas or even a little bit before. She warns me repeatedly not to share the information with anyone, even with Laci bácsi, afraid that somebody may find out about our forbidden radio.

My private lessons with Laci bácsi and Sara néni have started. I go to their house every day after school is over and do math, geography, history, and biology. "The basics!" says Laci bácsi. I like him better as a teacher than Sara néni. She is very nice, but when she comes home from school after teaching all morning, she is busy with her children, her cooking, and a lot of other chores. I don't feel she is giving me enough attention. Laci bácsi, on the other hand, explains everything in detail and wants to know if I don't understand something. He is patient and he always praises me for homework well done, especially mathematics, at which I seem to be very good.

"You'll be a scientist when you grow up," he says, laughing at me when I make a face. "Don't knock it. There are many pretty female scientists around these days."

CHAPTER FIVE

KISLÁNG

• Fall and Winter 1944 •

I T IS MID-OCTOBER AND something unexpected is happening. Mother hears it first on the big radio and hopes that it is true. It is announced by Regent Miklós Horthy that the Hungarian government has capitulated to the Allies and is no longer fighting on the side of the German forces. From now on, Hungary is going to be a neutral democracy and will not resist the advancing Russian Army or any of the Allies.

"If that is true," says Mother, "we can stop fearing so much for our lives and persecution by the Nazis or the Hungarian Arrow Cross. Let's hope that it is true."

We go outside and see that many of the village people must have heard the news too. They are walking up and down the road, and there is a lot of excited talking going on. Both Laci bácsi and Sara néni are very happy. They were never great friends of Hungary's alliance with Germany. Over coffee and cakes, there are discussions about how long it will take the Russians to overrun Hungary and reach the Austrian/German border, now that Hungarians are no longer participating in the fighting.

Late that afternoon, there is a shocking special announcement on the Hungarian radio that the German Army has forcibly removed Regent Horthy, and the new head of government is Ferenc Szálasi, the leader of the Arrow Cross. Szálasi declares that the Hungarian capitulation agreement of that morning is invalid and reinstates Hungary's affiliation with Germany. Any resistance to the new government is considered treason and reason for incarceration and death.

Suddenly, there is fear and silence all around. We go back to our house. Mother is very worried about what is going to happen next.

It is not yet quite dark when somebody rattles our gate. When we look out, we see a figure dressed in rags trying to get our attention. Mother almost screams for help, but then she puts her hand on her mouth and runs to the gate and drags the person inside, afraid that he might be seen. It is Pista, my stepfather. He is emaciated and dirty; his clothes are rags and his toes are visible through holes in his filthy shoes. Mother hugs him and he begins to cry. He mumbles hello to me. He sits down for a while without saying anything; tears are running down his face. Then he speaks to the sleeping Katika. "I am so happy to see you. I love you so much. Sometimes I didn't believe I would see you all again." He turns to me. "I love you too, Erika. What a beautiful big girl you have become."

I am having a hard time keeping my tears back. I am so glad that he is alive and I am so glad that Katika has a father.

Pista tells us that he spent close to a year on the German front in Russia digging ditches and performing menial labor for the Hungarian/German forces. But now the Army is in disarray, and he and another prisoner had escaped the retreating front lines. They set out to get back to Hungary on foot, following obscure routes among burnt out, mostly deserted villages at night.

That morning, October 15, 1944, he arrived in Budapest. Not finding us in our old apartment, he was desperate to know if we had been deported or killed. He went to my father's apartment, knowing that he would have information about us. Pista was with him when Regent Horthy announced Hungary's capitulation. Because of that news, my father felt free to tell Pista about our whereabouts and sent him immediately on his way to join us. Now that Hungary was no longer a German ally, it was safe for Pista to take the train. Father gave him the money and told him exactly where to find us. When Pista got off the train near Kisláng, he thought that there was nothing to fear. He walked the few kilometers to our house, not realizing that the infamous Ferenc Szálasi was now in power. When he arrived at our gate, happy and tired, he did not understand why Mother pulled him inside so anxiously.

Mother tells Pista that Szálasi is now in charge of the government. They realize that Pista has no identification or fake papers of any sort. He is now a fugitive from the Army's forced labor camp and a Jew. If he is spotted, he will be shot, and so will we. Mother decides to hide him. There is an attic in our little house that can be reached only by a ladder through a hole in the ceiling. Mother carries bedding, blankets, a bucket, and some water up the ladder. After Pista has a good meal, he climbs up the stairs and goes to sleep.

Mother sits down. She looks worried. "Do you realize how dangerous this could be for all of us?" she says to me. "We are now under a worse regime than we were before. Szálasi is known to be a raging anti-Semite, dedicated to collaborating with Germany in the extermination of the Jews. You have to be extra careful. I hope nobody heard Pista or saw him when he arrived, but we must pretend that he doesn't exist. We have to keep him secret, even from Katika, as much as possible. Although she does not speak a lot, she might give him away."

It is very difficult to live this way. Mother is nervous and yells at me a lot, and Katika has to be kept out of the house or out of the way any time that Pista comes down. Pista has dysentery and it is hard to keep him clean in the attic. Mother has to keep him out of sight when Varga bácsi comes to bring us food supplies. I have to make sure that neither Laci bácsi nor Sara néni find out anything about Pista's presence. "They are lovely people," says Mother, "but I don't think they would want to sacrifice their lives for us if the Arrow Cross found Pista in what is basically their house."

I spend a lot of time outside with Katika, but it's getting colder and it rains a lot. Mother wants me to take Katika with me when I go for my lessons so that Pista can come downstairs. But that is very difficult and I don't know how to explain it to Laci bácsi and Sara néni, so as usual Mother comes up with an acceptable lie, that she has a bad cold and does not want anybody to get it, especially Katika. They seem to accept that story. "What happens when you get better?" I ask. I don't like her answer. "They will have gotten used to Katika's presence at your lessons. I have to let Pista come down once in a while. I just have to."

One day, two soldiers are at the gate and want to come in. They are speaking German to Mother, who barely understands a word but manages to pretend she understands. The soldiers are very friendly. They tell her something about Vienna and Mother turns to me to say in Hungarian, "They found out that I am from Vienna and they decided to pay us a visit." I realize that she is warning me. They are officers of the German Army, stationed nearby and have come for a friendly visit. We have to play our

roles because Mother is known in town as the lady from Vienna.
I am pretty worried, but I don't say anything and smile. Pista in
the attic must hear them, I suppose, because all of a sudden, I
hear footsteps and so does Mother. Pista is pacing. Mother seems
scared, but only for a moment. She picks up Katika and holds
her in her arms. I can see clearly that she is pinching Katika's
behind forcefully. Katika wails and starts some serious crying. I
think the two officers look upset. They did not come to hear a
baby cry but to visit a pretty Austrian lady, and shortly, while
Katika is still wailing, they say goodbye and leave.

THE SOUND OF THE fighting on the front is getting closer. You
can hear cannon fire, and a lot of planes are flying over the village. Everybody is nervous and fearful. They are worried about
Russians occupying their village. They are afraid of the Russian
soldiers, who have a very bad reputation for looting and raping.

Mother says she is not too afraid. "For us," she says, "bad as
they may be, the Russians are the liberators. We will not have to
worry about the Nazis or the Arrow Cross taking us to a concentration camp. We will not have to remain in hiding."

There are plans being made on how to survive if a battle in
the village erupts between the retreating Germans and the advancing Russians. Judging by the number of planes and the
sound of the cannon fire, the fighting is close. Finally, in early
December, more and more deserting Hungarian soldiers pass
through the village, along with many other refugees telling horrible stories of the disintegrating front.

Varga bácsi says he no longer understands what is going on.
He curses, "Those damn Russians!" And in the next sentence he
says, "Those damn Germans!"

"Tell me, Varga bácsi," I ask him. "Which of them is worse?" He looks at me and says, "We know how bad one is and soon we will find out about the other."

The fighting is getting closer. When are the Russians finally going to be here? Some bombs fell in a nearby village, Varga bácsi tells us, and all of the roads are clogged with retreating German troops, their equipment, and refugees. The Russians are pushing the Germans more and more back toward the Austrian border, but in some of the villages there is fierce resistance.

"Most people are going to go to their cellars to be safe," says Varga bácsi. He means the potato cellars. There is one in almost every yard, usually behind the house, where winter supplies are also kept. They are dark, damp, and deep. "You can always dig out," says Laci bácsi, "if it collapses when hit."

I am no longer going for my lessons, and the school has closed too. Everybody is ready and waiting for the battle, preparing some food, bread and sausages, to take into the cellar. Our house does not have a potato cellar, so Laci bácsi and Sara néni assure us that their cellar is big enough and we can come stay with them. Just bring some nonperishable food and it will be fine, they say. Of course, this is a major dilemma because we cannot leave Pista in the attic or even in the house. Mother and Pista are having discussions about this in the evening when Katika is asleep, and Pista comes down. Pista offers to stay in the house when the battle starts.

When the fighting gets really bad and Laci bácsi comes across the street to fetch us to come to their cellar, Mother says, "Just a moment." She goes to get Pista from the attic. There is not much time for anyone to discuss or to protest. There are sirens blaring and planes dropping bombs. There is cannon fire close by. Laci bácsi takes one look at Pista and says, "Let's all go."

In the potato cellar, Laci bácsi turns to Pista and quietly asks, "You are Jewish, aren't you?" I am frozen in fear, looking at Mother for clues, not knowing whether the discovery of our Jewishness will put us in mortal danger. Mother is silent. Laci bácsi continues, "You must have been in a forced labor camp on the Russian front and escaped." Mother immediately picks up the conversation and with a charming smile says, "Yes, this is Pista Bakyoni, Katika's father. I am Mrs. Bakonyi, his wife, and the Austrian identity name of Nellie Bankuti you know me as is as fake as all of the other details of my and the children's background."

Sara néni says quietly, "You know, we suspected your secret all along."

Janos and Marta are playing cards quietly by candlelight, but it is obvious that they are listening to the conversation. Marta asks me, "What is your real name?" I am frightened and don't know what to say. I look at Mother for help and she says, "She's my daughter. Her name is Erika Bleier."

Sara néni turns to Marta and says, "Their names have changed. They are the same people as before."

Pista's smile is visible even in the faint candlelight of the dark cellar. "I am thankful that my family found safety with such wonderful human beings as you."

I'm thinking about when we come out of the cellar. Which name are we going to use? Am I going to be Bankuti or Bleier, the pretend or the real? I ask Mother but it is Sara néni who answers. "Maybe you all should keep your fake identity for a while because some of the village people might not understand."

Laci básci congratulates Pista on his escape from the forced labor camp and inquires about some details. I'm very glad that they seem to like each other because I do care for both of them very much. Mother and Sara néni are having a conversation about some cooked food when they get out of the cellar. I go and sit at a little table in the corner and join the card game with Janos and Marta.

We spend the next two days and nights in the potato cellar. Bombs are falling and exploding near us. I am hoping that they will not hit the cellar. The noise of the fighting at times is deafening: bombs and cannon fire. Both Laci bácsi and Pista know by the sound what weapons are being used, Pista especially since he was on the front for so long. Sometimes he tells us the make of the machine gun as it fires. By the end of the second day, the fighting seems to recede. Only occasional machine gunfire can be heard.

"They are here," whispers Laci bácsi. "When you can hear only machine guns, they are very close. I think it is also very dangerous. We don't want them to find us. Let's stay very quiet." But Katika doesn't listen. She wants to talk. Mother has some chocolate in her bag, and for the next couple of hours she stuffs chocolates in Katika's mouth every time she starts to make a sound.

We can hear some voices shouting and giving orders in Russian. After a while, when we don't hear voices any longer, Laci bácsi opens the door and we slowly go outside. We find Laci bácsi and Sara néni's house fully occupied by soldiers. The front rooms have all been requisitioned by officers. The little house across the street, where we have been staying, has been completely taken over by the Army. We go into Laci bácsi and Sara néni's house with them. The Russian soldiers seem friendly enough but point to Laci bácsi's wrist and motion for him to take off his watch. They seem satisfied with that and with a sweeping motion show us that we can stay in the kitchen and the room next to it. Laci bácsi and Sara néni tell us that we can stay with them. There will be eight of us in the two rooms.

Back in the kitchen, the adults are trying to organize who is going to sleep where. Pista suggests that we sleep in the kitchen and Laci bácsi and his family sleep in the other room. At first, this is accepted, but Sara néni changes all that. "The men, including Janos, should sleep in the kitchen to guard the door and all of us women should sleep in the other room. After all," she continues, "Marta looks about eighteen, although she only just turned thirteen years old—not that these soldiers care. I have heard that they kidnap and rape any woman, old or young, and some women never come back."

Rules are established. Janos, Marta and I are not to go in the yard without permission, unless accompanied by an adult. We have to wear several layers of clothing to cover our bodies. We are allowed to look dirty. We should not try to have a conversation with any of the soldiers. We are to be as invisible as possible.

I think the adults are overanxious. We don't hear any cannon fire or gunfire anymore, nor are planes flying overhead. "What are the big dangers in being seen?" I ask.

"First," says Mother, "we have two military-age men here. Any of the Russian soldiers may think that they are enemy troops. How do we explain that one was a teacher, exempt from the military, the other a Jewish refugee from a forced labor camp, lucky to survive German and Hungarian persecution?"

The first time Mother, Janos, and I leave the house to fetch some food from the cellar, we can see the road. We observe several horse-drawn carriages passing in front of the yard loaded up to the top. I see what is in the wagons and I scream. Mother too realizes that they are corpses and tries to shield my eyes, but it is too late. I've seen the dangling arms and the bobbing heads. "They must be from the battlefields," I say. "They are cleaning up." She drags Janos and me inside.

I'm shaking a bit and crying. I find it hard to stop. Mother is quiet, leaning against Pista, who is trying to comfort her while she wraps her arms around me. Janos is sitting at the table next to his mother and does not move. He is very pale and he looks like a statue. I'm not accustomed to being hugged and I am not comfortable with it, so I pull myself from my mother's embrace and sit down next to Janos at the table. "After dinner," I say, "do you want to play dominoes?"

"Can we play rummy instead?" He smiles and says, "I'm only kidding. We can play whatever you want."

Suddenly, there is motion at the door. A Russian officer is standing there. He is well-shaven and friendly looking. He surveys the kitchen, all of us sitting there, and says directly to Mother, "Yid?"

Mother is confused and asks Pista, "Does he want to know if we are Jewish?"

"He certainly looks Jewish himself, and means 'Jew' in Yiddish," Pista answers. He turns to the officer and speaks German to him. "Yes, we are Jewish," says Pista and waits for the reaction.

What follows is a conversation in a mixture of German and Yiddish that only they understand, but the results are surprising to us all. The officer tells Pista that we are too crowded and cannot be very comfortable, so he is going to give us back one more room in the house, next to the one we already have. He also allows us to go to the other house and fetch some of our clothing. He wants to know if Katika belongs to us and pats her on the head. He assures Pista that he is going to tell his men who are living in the front of the house not to bother us.

All of this is very good news. We can have an extra room, we can get our clothes from across the street, and his soldiers will not bother us too much. Soon, Mother and Pista fetch our things from the other house. We now have a whole room to ourselves, and all of us can use the kitchen for cooking, eating, and playing cards and dominoes.

WHEN PISTA FIRST REALIZED that the teachers' property is a farm, he is in total amazement. He was born and brought up in the city of Vienna and was not aware of the workings of a farm. But soon, he helps Laci bácsi gather food: eggs from the chicken coop and potatoes and other goodies from the potato cellar. He even helps milk the cows. Laci bácsi is careful to give a lot of the food to the Russian soldiers. "Men with full stomachs are less dangerous," he says. "Besides, it is much better to give it to them, because they will take it anyway."

Marta, Janos, and I stay mostly in the kitchen. We play dominoes and cards a lot and try to keep Katika from misbehaving. Everybody is getting restless. Mother is trying to keep busy mending some clothes. Sara néni cooks; Laci bácsi and Pista are in the fields. I am bored. There aren't many books around to read—they are all in the occupied rooms or have been thrown out by the soldiers to make room for their gear and guns. Laci bácsi is too busy trying to keep the farm alive to give me lessons like he used to. We listen to Hungarian radio, which is still transmitting "happy news" from the front that the German and Hungarian armies have recovered and are back on the march to recapture lost territory. Nobody is certain that they are hearing the truth, but one day the noise of cannon fire is coming from the west, signifying that the battle is nearing. Mother, Pista, Laci bácsi, and Sara néni are debating the situation every moment. I am playing innumerable games of cards and dominoes to pass the time.

"If the Germans come back, we are going to be the first ones to be killed," says Mother.

Pista disagrees. "I don't think it will happen," he says. "The Germans were beaten already when I escaped the camp. I don't believe they can gather their forces and recapture this part of the country."

Sara néni agrees with Pista, but Laci bácsi is not so sure. "I don't think," he says, "the village people will give you up, although the news has spread of Pista's presence, and I heard them say that you are Jewish. If the Germans really come back," he continues, "we'll have to see where we can hide you."

"It won't be possible," says Mother. "If somebody in this village wants to give us up, they will find us. There is always somebody. If the Germans come any closer, we will have to leave."

PISTA, SARA NÉNI, AND Laci básci are out into the fields to gather some firewood. I overheard that there were some other treasures—money and jewelry—buried there so they wouldn't be stolen or "requisitioned," as it is called by the Russian soldiers. Today, they were going to dig up some actual money from a field.

Marta is allowed for the first time since the occupation to visit a girlfriend. Janos is out in the garden doing some cleanup. Katika is playing quietly and is about to fall asleep. Mother decides that this is a good time for me to get cleaned up. We pour some warm water into the basin on the washstand. I take off my old shirt which is made of a flannel-like material. It is very dirty. I don't think it is going to survive another washing. My undershirt, on the other hand, is still holding up. We have washed it many times and it still has no holes. I take that off too. I put the blouse and the undershirt to the side and feel really naked. I am ten years old and not used to my budding breasts. I bend over the basin when Mother realizes that she wants to wash my hair. She goes to find some petroleum to mix with the water. It is supposed to prevent or kill head lice.

Meanwhile, I enjoy feeling the water on my body, but what is this? Who is pushing me from the back? I want to turn, but I cannot. Someone is holding me down and lying on top of me so that I cannot move. The basin tips and water spills out over the top. I am trying to free myself but I cannot move. Now, there is a hand covering my mouth, and I am pinned down by the sheer weight of what I think must be one of the soldiers. I feel the buttons of his uniform pressing into my behind. He has already pulled back my underwear.

I have heard a lot about what soldiers did to women and girls. But I do not know what it actually is. What horrible thing do they do to girls? I have wanted to ask my mother because she doesn't want me to leave the house at all. And when she, who is very beautiful, goes out, she puts ashes on her face to look older. Mother also wears many layers of clothes to hide her body. When she goes out, she looks very unattractive.

I am motionless. I don't dare to breathe. What is happening? Then I hear a horrifying scream: It is Mother cursing and yelling at the top of her lungs. Suddenly I am let go. I turn around, covering my breasts, and I see the young soldier whom Mother has pulled off my back standing in the middle of the room. Now that he is no longer threatening me, Mother raises her hand and smacks his face hard, right, left, and right again with a tirade of angry words.

"You imbecile, what were you thinking? Aren't you ashamed of yourself? What would your mother say if she saw you? Your mother would beat you up. You dirty scum of the earth. She is merely a child, and so are you." Under my mother's words, the soldier, who is a tall guy, becomes a shrunken little boy. He doesn't speak Hungarian, and I am certain he does not actually understand a word she is saying, but he hears the tone. He understands everything my mother says by the force of her words.

She turns to me and says, "Are you hurt?" I say, "No. I was scared and uncomfortable not being able to move. I did not know what was happening and didn't like when he put his hand over my mouth."

Laci bácsi, hears the commotion, as he comes into the house. He looks around and gets the picture. He screams at my mother, "God almighty! Don't you know the danger you put us into? That guy has a gun. He could have shot all of us."

"But he didn't, did he?" Mother replies and smiles.

The soldier is still standing in the corner of the room with his head hanging in shame. His face is red from the slaps he received from my mother. He is bent over as he shuffles slowly toward the door of the kitchen. He looks afraid somebody will actually beat him up. As he leaves, I think he looks like an old, old man.

RUMORS INCREASE OF KILLINGS and looting by the Russians. It is dangerous to walk in the streets. You may never get home. Nobody wears watches anymore, but the soldiers walk around with all of the watches they have taken, lined up from their wrists to their upper arms. Varga bácsi no longer visits. We have no news of my grandmother, who is only a couple of houses away. Laci bácsi continues to keep the soldiers living in his house content with gifts of milk, eggs, bread, and even an occasional chicken. But the soldiers don't do a lot of cooking anymore because there is a field kitchen in one of the houses nearby for all of the soldiers occupying the village. They ring the church bell twice a day when their meals are ready.

The grown-ups try to go about their business attending to the animals and milking their cows whenever possible. Laci bácsi's horses have been requisitioned. We don't know where the soldiers take them in the morning, but they come home at night to their stables. They are dirty and haven't been fed and Laci bácsi suspects that they have been beaten.

We don't get much news of the progression of the war, but there are stories that the advance of Russian troops toward Germany has slowed down. There is more talk of the possibility that the Germans may reoccupy the village. I feel the fear all around me. Everyone is upset and nervous.

Katika has developed a nasty diarrhea, probably as a result of all of the chocolate she ate in the cellar. Mother and I are constantly washing diapers, made of old sheets and blankets, trying to keep things clean. Janos and Marta are obnoxious. They fight with each other, tease me a lot, and are generally a nuisance. Pista is trying to help Laci bácsi on the property. But every time they go outside, we cannot be sure of them coming back. The Russians are collecting men in the village to help them with burying the dead and other tasks.

One morning, there are two Russian soldiers standing at our kitchen door, guns drawn. They do not look friendly. Mother clutches me tightly and picks up Katika, but these soldiers do not smile. They are bent on business. Laci bácsi and his family are out in the fields doing chores. The soldiers herd the four of us out the door and line us up with about a dozen other men and women against a long wall at the side of the house.

"I'm afraid this is it," Pista says, but I can barely hear him. I'm not sure what he means, but I'm scared that I do. Soldiers lining people up against a wall means they are going to shoot. Mother, next to me, is shaking and holding me so tightly it hurts. Katika, in her arms, is for once quiet. Pista stands on Mother's other side and has his arm around her shoulder. I'm not sure if he wants to protect her or wants to make sure he does not collapse. One shot is fired. I look before Mother's hand reaches across my head and covers my eyes. Someone at the end of the line has fallen. There are screams, but I am not sure where they come from. I can feel some pee dripping down my leg. Then there is another shot, another thump, more screams. Somebody is praying aloud. Now all of us are facing the wall. I am waiting for the next shot but instead I hear a bell. The church bell is ringing, calling the soldiers to the field kitchen for lunch. All the soldiers turn, and carrying their guns, they leave to get their lunch.

We stand there for quite a while. The people at the end of the line, next to those who were shot, are attending to them. I am not sure but I think they are dead. We don't dare to move. I want to go inside but Mother says, "Wait one more minute."

"No," I say. "I don't want to be here when they come back."

When we go inside, we collapse at the kitchen table and hold on to one another. I am tired. I don't want to hear anybody speak. I put my head on my arms on the table and hope to fall asleep. Instead, I go elsewhere. I hear my Grandmother Adél's voice in my mind. She says, "Be careful. The soup is hot." I'm at the dinner table at my grandparents' house. It is Friday night. We are sitting around the table having listened to my cousin Tom

reciting from the Torah, a part that he will read at the synagogue
tomorrow. It is his bar mitzvah. "That was wonderful, young
man," says my grandfather. "I am proud of you. But I hope you
don't get carried away with yourself." My Aunt Erzsi, who is
also there, adores her son and her pride shows. I can see a tear
in her eye and Uncle Laci too looks happy. My cousin Marika
is snuggling up to her father. She is trying to tell me something
but is sitting too far from me to understand. Still we laugh and
giggle, holding our little secrets to exchange later. I am very
happy that my cousins are here. Grandmother Adél is busy, serving dinner and making sure that everybody has more than
enough on their plates. She smiles at me from across the table to
let me know that I am still her special grandchild. My mother,
sitting next to me, does not seem to enjoy the celebration and
suddenly pushes my elbow off of the table. "It's ill-mannered to
eat that way," she says.

The noise of the door opening brings me back to the reality
of our situation. I realize that Sara néni, Laci bácsi, and their
children have returned from the fields. They say that they heard
about the shooting. It seems the Russian soldiers were looking
for a fugitive of the Hungarian Army, a high-ranking officer,
who was supposed to be hiding in this part of the country.

"Other people say that a man resisted being taken away to
work for them," reports Laci bácsi. "Some soldiers got angry and
decided to shoot several men and their families to teach them a
lesson. There is also talk about the progress of the war, which is
not going too well right now for the Russians. The Germans
have been making concentrated efforts to regain some of the
territory."

I really don't want to listen. I really don't want to think about
it. I know that if the Germans come back, they will kill us.

Maybe they won't even put us against the wall like the Russians did; maybe they will just shoot us straight from the kitchen door.

LATER IN THE DAY our friend, the Russian officer, pays us a visit. He obviously knows that his men almost killed us and that they did kill two innocent men. He doesn't say very much, but he does explain in his broken German-Yiddish to Pista that the fighting is coming closer to the village. When he leaves, Pista says that he probably meant the visit to be an apology of sorts and a warning.

"Do you realize," says Pista, "that we will have to leave before the Germans get here?"

"How are we going to get away?" asks Mother.

There is no answer to that question. The gloom in the kitchen is heavy and we all decide to go to sleep. During the night, the noise of the fighting is fierce. There are loud explosions, the drone of fighter planes, and the bang-bang of cannon fire.

CHAPTER SIX

KISLÁNG TO BALATONKENESE

• January 1945 •

THE RUSSIAN OFFICER, OUR protector, is back in the morning. "I don't like it," Pista says when he sees him approaching. "I don't like the expression on his face. I don't think he is bringing good news." Pista is right. The officer proceeds to explain that the Russian Army is retreating to wait for supplies, allowing the German Army to temporarily recapture this territory. The German Army is fast approaching and it is clear that it will reoccupy the village shortly.

"We have been listening to bombs exploding and cannon fire all night," says Mother. "He doesn't have to tell us how close they are." But the officer has no time for conversation. He has an agenda.

"In ten minutes," he explains in his broken German and with the help of his hands, "I am coming back to get you. You are retreating with us, the Russian Army, to avoid being killed by the Nazis. Be ready."

Mother grabs our battered suitcase, some food, and whatever else she can find and packs it in the suitcase. I want to say goodbye to Laci bácsi and his family but there is no time. The officer arrives in a horse-drawn buggy, followed by another horse-drawn carriage fully loaded with supplies and two soldiers riding on it.

"God!" says Mother when she sees the buggies. "Where did he find those?"

The horses are dirty and skinny and the buggies do not look too good either.

"Never mind," says Pista anxiously. "Hurry up. If they get us out of here in time, we might escape another German occupation alive."

When we come out of the house, the village seems quiet. Everyone has moved back to the potato cellars because of the approaching battle. Much of the Russian Army has already left. We climb on the buggy and Pista takes the reins. "Go east," says our Russian friend. "Follow the other buggy and head for the Danube. The main highway will be clogged with a lot of retreating tanks and soldiers. They too are moving in the direction of the Danube. Stay away from the main roads," he cautions. "Those two soldiers know the way to a dirt road that I think will be safer."

We leave the village on a path through the fields, following the buggy with the two soldiers and going east as instructed. The dirt road we are traveling on is narrow and deserted—no sign of tanks or soldiers and no low-flying Stukas, German bombers. There are three parallel roads leading east. The Russian Army, retreating on the main road to our right, is ahead of us. The Germans, who are advancing from the west, are behind us. Our road is in the middle of two armies. It is deserted and uneven with deep ruts, but we are making fair progress following the lead buggy.

As darkness falls, the battle erupts again. Planes overhead are dropping flares to illuminate the area; bombs and cannon fire are whistling through the air and exploding nearby with ear-shattering bangs. The Russians are protecting their retreat with heavy artillery fire to keep the Germans at bay, while the advancing German Army is attacking with all the might they can still muster. Our horse shies from the lights and the noise and starts to pull on the buggy, causing it to rock. I clutch Mother's arm to steady myself and try to help her keep Katika safe in her arms. Pista gets off the carriage and tightens the horse's rein to prevent the frightened animal from panicking.

The fighting is coming closer and the artillery fire, going in both directions, is right over our heads. I watch the fast-moving yellow streaks against the dark sky, fascinated. They create strange geometric patterns of crosses, rectangles, and squares. The explosions on the impact of cannon fire and bombs cause flashes of multicolored fire. Still holding on to Mother, I am enthralled by the incredible display.

"We are in the middle of a battlefield with nowhere to hide," says Mother, stating the obvious. There are no trees, no protection, just a dirt road surrounded by wide open spaces. The soldiers in the buggy ahead of us notice that we have stopped and they stop too. Shortly, we start to move again and follow the leading buggy.

"I can see some trees ahead of us," says Mother. "Would it not be safer to stop there?"

"No," Pista answers. "We have to follow the lead carriage. We don't want to get lost and end up on the main road."

We are passing the trees when the carriage in front of us receives a full hit. The impact nearly turns our buggy upside down. The explosion is unbearably loud, and the fire it creates instantly robs me of my eyesight for a moment. Our horse gets scared and jumps, almost upsetting the wagon. I hold on to the bench and to my mother and manage to stay on my seat. I hear things falling around us, and my vision slowly returns. In the blinding light, I see Pista divert a piece of smoldering wood with a bare hand to prevent it from hitting the horse. The wagon in front of us is fully ablaze.

Mother's scream is loud and frightened. It is scary. I look over at her, and in that menacing light of the burning carriage, I see Mother clutching Katika and pulling away from a strange object that has landed next to her. It is bloody and barely recognizable, except for the boot—I can tell it is a badly mangled leg. My own scream freezes in my throat as I watch Mother pick up the leg by the frayed fabric of what were once trousers and toss it over the side of the carriage. Then I turn to see the other soldier standing on my side of the wagon with his arm stretched up reaching toward me. Frightened, I pull back. I don't want to be touched. But I see that he is crying. I watch a giant teardrop sliding down his face. He almost touches me, but suddenly he reels back and slowly slumps to the ground. I realize as he is falling that what I thought was a giant teardrop was not a tear at all but was in fact one of the soldier's eyes.

"He's dead," Mother says, turning to me, "and we have to move on. The fire is bright. We have become too visible a target."

Pista picks up a sack of potatoes and some undamaged food scattered around, spilled by the explosion. He puts it in our carriage, and then he gathers the reins and coaxes the frightened old horse into motion.

"Don't look," he says to me as we pass around the smoldering wreckage. But it is too late. I see the corpse, lying facedown on the ground, one leg missing. It is blocking our passage. Pista does not stop. He pulls the horse and the carriage over the body and we continue east on the narrow dirt road. The fighting around us appears to move closer and seems to become even more ferocious than before.

"Where are we going?" Mother moans. "We should not be out in such open territory. We have to find shelter."

Without the lead carriage, we have lost our sense of direction. But we keep going, following the dirt road, our rickety vehicle protesting with shudders and sighs. The ancient horse is moving but very slowly. I am wondering if the horse will die before the carriage falls apart or if the carriage will disintegrate first.

Pista stops. "There are some trees to the left and a wide path," he says. "It must lead to a house of some sort. Shall we try to go that way?"

"Yes," Mother agrees. "Anything is better than staying on this road."

The path is long and winding and leads to a large house. Pista knocks and the door soon opens. The man who stands in the doorway can see us illuminated by the light of the floating flares dropped by the planes. The inside of the house is completely dark due to the strictly enforced blackout.

"Tie up your horse over there with the others and then come in," he directs.

When the door closes behind us, the man lights an oil lamp. He is dressed in clean clothes and shiny shoes. He introduces himself as the administrator of the estate of a well-known and well-respected aristocratic family. We are in his home on the premises of the estate. Behind him we see a large room with many people, mostly women and children, some eating, others lying on the floor sleeping, still others are sitting wherever space is available, tending to each other and their children.

"All the people here," the man says, "arrived in the last few days hungry, bombed out of their homes, fleeing from the fighting, fearing the Russians or the Germans, the bombs, the artillery, and the tanks. Others are probably deserters from the Hungarian Army who have realized that the fighting will soon be over because the war is lost, and they want to stay alive. No matter what," he continues, "I have some supplies left and consider it my duty to shelter and feed as many people as possible, regardless of who they are or what they are afraid of. Please, eat something. Find a spot to sit or lie down and sleep."

He points to a sideboard along the wall with food: bread, cheese, salami, and milk. First, we clean up as best we can in a real bathroom, although there is no warm water. Then we help ourselves to some food, but no matter how I try, Katika won't eat. Mother no longer nurses her and Katika has a hard time handling the food we have. I don't like the way she looks and acts. I'm worried that she might be sick. Finally, we settle down in a corner to sleep. An angry bang on the door shocks us awake.

"Machen Sie auf!" demands a loud and dangerous voice in German. (*Open up!*)

My mother clutches me and freezes when she hears the order from the German soldier. She gives barely audible directives to us. "Do not talk. Do not say anything, no matter what they ask. Leave the talking to me."

But the group of soldiers who enter are not interested in asking questions or demanding identification papers. They look around at the sad collection of refugees and realize that no Russian soldiers are hiding among us. They themselves are battle-weary, dirt-covered, leery, and hungry.

"Sprechen Sie Deutsch?" one of them says to no one in particular. (*Do you speak German?*)

Before Mother can stop him, Pista volunteers, "Ja bitte, ich bin Österreicher." (*Yes please, I am Austrian.*)

"Gut," says the soldier who seems to be in charge. Pista listens to rapid German instructions and proceeds to tell us what is being said. "The German Army has overnight recaptured this part of the country. They do not intend to cause harm to anyone, but they want to remind us that they will shoot anyone if they find them harboring the enemy."

I'm wondering what they mean—Russian soldiers, Russian defectors, Jews of any sort, or Hungarian defectors? I don't think they are really interested in the enemy. I think what they want to do is frighten us. They want us to give up the food without a fight.

"They want the administrator's supplies," says Pista.

He continues to converse with the soldiers, who show no sign of asking for his papers. Pista accompanies them as they check the whole house for "enemies" and search for food. No enemies are discovered, but they do find a lot of potatoes and corn, which seems to satisfy them as they proceed to load the loot into a military truck parked in front of the door.

When Pista returns to where we are sitting, he is nervous and agitated. "They want me to accompany them to nearby villages as their interpreter. They want me to be the intermediary between the Hungarian villagers and themselves. They want to find some of the food that is known to be hidden, like smoked sides of beef, ribs, and other preserved meats, besides the potatoes and the corn that is in plain sight. They want me to convince the villagers to give it to them."

There is a moment of shocked silence and then Mother asks, "What about us?"

"You can come along as long as you realize that you will be sleeping in a military truck. We will be heading west, farther away from Kisláng and lessening the chance of running into anyone who knew us there as Jews," he adds in a low whisper.

"What about papers?" Mother asks. "Did they not ask you for your ID? Did they not want to know why you are here and not in the Army?"

"I told them that one of our bags burned when the other wagon was hit. My papers were in that bag. I told them that I was on medical leave, visiting my family, when we were overrun by the Russians. I offered them your papers to prove my identity, but they said it was not necessary. They needed me to interpret with Hungarians, and besides, I was Austrian and therefore I was a friend." Pista smiles, oddly hesitates, and then continues, "I made sure that I peed next to the commander, letting him see my uncircumcised penis so he would not think I could be Jewish."

"Let's go," says Mother, gathering Katika and our small suitcase with all of our possessions. "The farther we get away from Kisláng, the safer we will be."

We climb into the back of the Germans' truck, leaving behind the kindly administrator and the dilapidated wagon we had arrived in. I saw that our horse had mercifully died during the night and was now lying on his back at the far end of the yard, four legs stiffly pointing up at the gray sky. It is getting noticeably colder and it is going to snow.

We leave the estate in the Germans' truck. The first village we come to is in ruins and deserted. The burned-out houses on both sides of the road offer little in the way of food or shelter. The small convoy our truck is a part of heads toward a main road going north. Sitting in the back of the truck, I have a full view of everything we pass. The road is littered with the debris of the previous night's battle: burned-out tanks, Russian or German, so black you can't tell the difference by their markings. The dead bodies are more easily recognizable by their uniforms, although some of them are badly burned too.

We spend the next three days with the German soldiers in their truck. All communications between them and their headquarters have broken down. They are desperately trying to find their commander or any commander, but without any success. Their radios do not work, nor can they be sure of being on German-occupied soil or having unwittingly crossed into Russian territory. They speak freely to Pista of how little hope they have left of winning the war. It is obvious that the German Army is falling apart. They take Pista with them to every village we stop in to try to find food, but the villages are mostly burned down and deserted. Occasionally, they find a few old or sick people who are just as hungry as we are. We survive on stale bread, some potatoes, onions, corn, and eggs.

Mother is getting increasingly worried every time Pista accompanies the Germans into a village and we have to stay in the truck waiting. Sometimes we hear gunfire. Mother screams and starts to tremble until Pista comes back.

"We have to get away from them," she says to Pista, "before they ask us for papers and realize that we are Jewish." Pista agrees. He has noticed a change in the Germans' attitude but he is not sure why. Mother says, "I know what to do. I have a plan." She looks at me and tells me not to get too upset with what she is going to do.

That night, it starts to snow and it turns bitter cold. In the morning, Mother wakes up bent over. She is clutching her stomach, whimpering and crying. She says she can't straighten up because the pain in her belly is so intense. Her fake appendicitis attack is so well acted, so real, that the soldiers become frightened and decide that she has to be brought to the nearest hospital. We drive around for another day trying to get to a hospital, Mother carrying on convincingly all the time. There is no food, nor is the back of the truck sheltered from the biting cold.

"We are approaching Lake Balaton," says one of the soldiers. "When we get to the first village, we will let you get out. There is a Hungarian hospital there. It is marked on our map."

A few minutes later, they stop the truck and point up the hill. "The hospital is only a couple of steps from the road."

They drive away as soon as we get off the truck. A battered sign on the side of the road barely hanging on its post reads *Balatonkenese*. For a while we wander around, my mother upright, miraculously cured, looking for shelter. It has stopped snowing but it is getting colder. The wind blowing in from the lake is penetrating and cruel. Balatonkenese, in the late afternoon of this frigid January day, seems completely deserted. No villagers nor German soldiers are to be seen. We are freezing, hungry, and desperate.

Mother points to a ditch on the side of the road. "This will protect us somewhat from the wind."

CHAPTER SEVEN

BALATONKENESE

• 1945, the Coldest Winter •

W E HUDDLE IN THE ditch, the four of us, as close to each other as possible. It is cold—all-pervasive, bone-chilling cold. We are trying to preserve the heat of our bodies, trying to avoid contact with the ice at the bottom of the ditch, trying to protect the exposed areas of our bodies from the cold and the wind. Our clothing affords little protection, consisting mostly of torn and threadbare bits of old sweaters, pieces of a blanket, and several layers of newspaper wrapped around the holes in our shoes or stuffed inside our clothes to prevent the wind from blowing in.

Our faithful companion—a small, battered suitcase that carries our meager supplies—lies next to my mother on the ice at the bottom of the ditch and is empty. But I'm not hungry. I am looking up at the sky thinking how close it seems to be, close enough so that I can almost touch it. It is a beautiful dark, velvety blue, and millions of little gold stars are blinking brightly, as if they are sending signals to each other. The blackout, which is enforced all over the country, prevents the planes from finding targets for their bombs, but it allows the moonlight to shine brighter and to illuminate the landscape magically. It is quiet—no planes, no bombs, no gunfire. As the cold spreads more and more through our bodies, not even the beauty of the night can ease a sense of doom taking hold. Mother's grip on me tightens. "We are going to freeze to death here," she says. She starts to rock back and forth repeating over and over again, "How did this happen to us? How did we get here? And how are we going to stay alive?" Her voice fades but I can still feel her holding on to me.

In the ditch a faint sound disrupts our apathy. As it gets stronger, Pista becomes alert. "I don't believe it," he whispers. "It sounds like a violin. It's Mozart! Somebody is playing Mozart on the violin."

I look toward the source of the sound and see what looks like a black cutout against the moonlight, a figure in what seems to be a German uniform playing the violin and walking down the deserted road toward us. Pista's love of music takes over and he starts to whistle a harmony to the soldier's tune. Mother's fingers tighten on my shoulder and she whispers, angry and frightened, "Pista, for the love of god, stop, don't whistle. Oh god, can't you see? It's a soldier and he will discover us!"

But Pista does not stop whistling, nor does the soldier stop playing his violin. When he reaches a spot on the road just above our ditch, they finish the tune in unison. Silence follows until the soldier speaks. "Do you speak German?" Pista answers in his impeccable Viennese accent. "Yes, I'm Austrian." I cannot comprehend the conversation that follows, but I feel my mother relax and I understand that this is not a threatening encounter.

I am confused. How come this particular soldier is not dangerous? How come in spite of his uniform we are not running away from him, like we frequently do on other occasions when we see German soldiers? How come we are climbing out of the ditch and following him toward his quarters in the village? "He wants to put us up for the night," Pista says. "He is going to tell the owner of the house that we are relatives from Vienna living in Budapest, but are now staying nearby trying to escape the bombardments in the city." But mother isn't interested in talking. "Does he have some food?" she asks. Pista ignores her question. "We're not too far from his quarters."

Pista, emaciated and shivering in his rags, walks and talks up front with the soldier. Mother, moving with difficulty after several hours in the ditch, is carrying Katika, who is weak and traumatized and no longer speaks or cries. My attention wanders; I look around to the lake on the left and to the houses on the right—a row of cottages, many bombed out or damaged by gunfire from the battles that took place in the area. The bare wintry trees lining the road show battle scars as well—broken limbs and missing crowns are clearly visible in the moonlight. The road we are walking on is free of debris, kept clean by the army so that tanks can pass, but piled up on the side there are heaps of refuse from bomb-damaged homes and burnt-out trucks.

The soldier's quarters are in a villa, severely damaged by the bombardment, on a side street just a few steps up from the main road. He tells us that the villa is owned by a local woman. What passes as his room is in the front of the house and must at one time have been the veranda. It had its own entrance and many windows, but the glass in most of them has been blown out by nearby explosions. Black paper or oilcloth is taped to replace the glass and to keep the wind out and the light in.

The soldier goes in first and puts on a small oil lamp to show us the way. The space is large but has very little furnishings: one bed, a folding table, and two chairs. There is no heat, no electricity, no water. The outhouse is a few steps up the hill in the yard and consists of a bench with a hole cut in it over a pit, enclosed by a few rickety planks. The door does not close, and one can see out as well as in through the openings between the planks. In the soldier's room there are some leftovers on the table— some bread and a little ham. The soldier motions for us to sit down and eat. Then he says something to Pista and leaves.

"He went to get some blankets and some more food, and to try to find some milk for Katika."

"Thank god," said Mother. "I don't think Katika will survive much longer without milk."

Pista is silent. I can see that he has tears in his eyes. But he does not respond to Mother's remark. When he speaks, his voice is hoarse. "He's not just a soldier," he says, "but a high-ranking commanding officer, the highest in this area. He's on leave for as long as the front stays quiet, probably only a few more days. He believes that most of the army knows that the war is lost. But they have orders to continue to fight to prevent the Russians from reaching and crossing the border of Austria. Another Russian offensive is expected." He pauses, then continues. "By the way, he is also an accomplished violinist who plays first violin with one of the best Viennese orchestras."

Mother isn't impressed. "We have to have water to clean up," she says. "We also have to find out what the woman who owns this house is like. She might report us to the authorities for the small reward offered to those who turn in Jews. We must find out about her. And you, Erika, you better keep quiet if she asks you any questions. Just act dumb." She didn't have to tell me that. She has said it a hundred times before.

Mother, Katika, and I sleep in the bed that night, while Pista and the soldier sleep on some blankets on the floor. I wake up to the smell of food the next morning. On the table are a loaf of bread, butter, smoked bacon, and a large pitcher of milk. Mother is busy trying to feed Katika some bread dunked into the milk.

"Come and eat," she says when she notices that I am awake. "There is plenty of food and the soldier is going to bring more. The man is a miracle. Look there in the corner—he brought a washstand with a basin and a bucket with warm water already in it. You can wash up after you eat," she continues, "but be careful."

"Careful of what?" I want to ask. But asking her questions has become useless. Lately, she is quick to answer with her hands, usually across my face or back. Still, I can think of many more things I want to ask. *Mother, why are you so short-tempered? Why don't you tell me something nice? Why don't you tell me just how well I learned to keep quiet, how helpful I am doing everything you tell me to do, how I am not complaining of the cold, the hunger, or the fear?* Mostly, I want to ask her about my little sister: *What has happened to Katika? Why does she no longer speak? Why has she stopped crying? Mother, you can trust me. I'm a big girl now. I'm ten years old and I wish you would answer some of my questions.* But I don't ask. I know better. Just then, her voice interrupts my thoughts.

"You are daydreaming again," she says. She put some old newspapers in front of me and hands me a knife. "Cut these into squares," she instructs, "and take them to the latrine with you when you go." When I look at her questioningly, she says, "It is better than no paper at all." She then points to a second pile of newspapers and tells me to cut them into bigger sheets. Katika, who was completely toilet-trained back in Kisláng, has been soiling herself, and Mother is going to use the bigger pieces of paper to line her underwear. The soldier has promised that morning to try to get some cotton or gauze from the medical unit to be used instead as diapers, but he has not come back yet.

The day passes slowly. The soldier has taken Pista with him. "We are lucky," Mother says. "Pista's good looks and gentile appearance prevent even the most fervent of the Arrow Cross Jew hunters to ask him for his ID." I've spent the morning playing with Katika on the floor, trying to wake her from her apathetic state. Since she was born, I have helped to take care of her—I fed her, I changed her, I bathed her, I walked her, and I taught her to speak. We used to have fun playing games and she used to follow me around like a puppy dog. Her silence and unresponsiveness frighten me, but after a while that morning, she smiles and makes little sounds. "What is the matter with her?" I think.

"Do you think she will be all right?" I ask Mother. "Of course she will," she answers.

Mother calls me to come and sit on the bed with her. I know what she is going to do and I want to protest, "Mother, please, don't open my braids, don't comb my hair, please don't, please don't look for lice, please don't pull my hair." But out loud I only say, "Be careful, it hurts." She takes pride in finding the lice. She pulls them one by one from my hair and then she shows me each tiny dark speck, no larger than the head of a pin. She places it on the nail of her left thumb and squashes it with the nail of her right thumb, accompanied by a deep sigh of satisfaction.

Pista and the soldier return with a lot of goodies, mostly food, oil for the lamps, and more blankets. Mother is worried because Katika seems to have a fever. Mother decides to approach the owner of the house in the kitchen to ask her for boiling water to make compresses for Katika's chest. We hear a scream. It is

Mother. She tells us that the lady was so nasty to her about using the kitchen that Mother got upset and spilled the boiling water on her right arm. Mother is in pain. With the help of the soldier, we bandage her arm with some newspaper and string.

After we eat, the soldier takes his violin and goes for a walk. Pista smiles and says, "The cold spell is over. His violin will sound much better tonight." Then he turns serious. "The Russians have started a new offensive to recapture the area. The German Army is falling apart; communications have broken down in many units. Supplies have not come in and there are many deserters. Still, there will be serious fighting before this area is recaptured. Dangerous battles are expected before the Russians will liberate us again."

"We are not leaving here," Mother says. "We are not going anywhere. We are staying here until the war ends."

My confusion deepens as I listen to all of this. Who are we afraid of now? Our soldier is good to us, but he is a German. The Russian officer in Kisláng, who gave us the buggy to escape the Germans, was a good guy too. Some of the Hungarians we encountered would have killed us if they had known we were Jewish, yet they let us into their homes because we needed a place to sleep. So, who are our friends and who are our enemies? Who knows the answers?

The soldier is called back the next morning to join his unit. As we are saying our goodbyes, Pista turns to Mother and says, "You know, he told the woman who owns the house that we are staying. I was translating for him when he said it. He also said to her that he would hold her personally responsible if anything happened to us." Obviously, he was getting as fond of us as we are of him.

Shortly after the soldier leaves, the bombardment resumes.

The sound of cannon fire is coming closer and closer. For the next few days, we try to ration our food. Pista is sick. His dysentery has returned. He looks weak and dejected. We do not leave our room and just wait. Mostly we are silent, but occasionally, Mother will muse, "Are we still under the German occupation? Or is it the Russians now?"

"I don't know; I really don't know," Pista answers. "I guess it is the Germans still. No Russian soldiers have checked the house yet." We continue waiting and hoping that our quarters will not receive a direct hit from the next wave of bombardments.

Two or three more days pass. One morning there is a lull in the fighting and Pista says, "I'm going out. I need to find out what has happened. I also need to find some food." The protest from my mother is feeble. We need food.

Pista returns sooner than expected. He stands in the doorway leaning against the frame. He looks broken, shattered. I think he is about to fall, but he doesn't. He just stands there. When Mother sees him, she screams, "Oh, no, no, no!" and she screams again. Still looking at Pista, her voice breaks and she whispers, "It is the soldier, isn't it?"

"His tank took a full hit yesterday. He is dead."

CHAPTER EIGHT

BALATONKENESE

• 1945 •

THE SILENCE LASTS A long time. Mother's voice, when she speaks, is raspy and low. She is sad and angry and about to cry. "Those damn Germans," she says. "They want to fight until they kill the best of us and of them, and we, the innocents, suffer."

She is really angry now, lamenting our fate. Her voice is shrill and getting louder. "Our protector is gone. We don't have food. Pista is sick." She is reciting all of our woes, again and again. I too feel like crying for the soldier, and for us, but I don't dare. I am afraid her anger will turn on me, as it often does. I don't want to listen. She is yelling. I do not want to hear what she is saying. I want to hear something nice. I want to go elsewhere. I hear my grandmother Kato néni's voice calling me for breakfast.

"Erikám, édesem (*my sweet Erika*), look! We are having your favorite: crisp, white rolls, sliced goose liver, and kakao (*chocolate milk*) to drink!"

I am in the garden of her summer house in Balatonlelle. She calls me again.

"Come, my sweet, and start to eat!"

I am busy observing a butterfly with multicolored wings sitting on a white flower, and I do not want to go to the porch where Ilonka, her housekeeper, had set the breakfast table. Kato néni calls again, this time singing her words—lovely, endearing words to the well-known tune of an operatic aria: "You with the beautiful eyes, la la la la. They light up like stars in the night in your lovely face, la la la la. I love you my little one. Tra la la la la. Now come and eat!"

She does not wait for me to obey. She comes closer and scoops me up, takes me to the table, and sits down with me to eat. I love being on her lap. Her bulk surrounds me and makes me feel safe.

I am still in her garden. I see her face and hear her song. But it fades. The voice I hear now is the screeching, angry voice of my mother.

"What's the matter with you? Can't you hear me? I've been talking to you! Were you daydreaming again? You have to stop that nonsense! You have to listen! We can't go on like this. We have to do something! We have to get some food!"

She is pacing around the room and I, as if waking from a dream, follow her with my eyes and see Pista on the bed, so weakened by dysentery and lack of food that he cannot get up, and Katika, lying on a blanket on the floor, soundless and looking very, very sick. Mother is going around in circles, muttering now, saying to no one in particular: "I have been looking everywhere for food. Not a crumb, not even on the floor!" She repeats this many times, walking faster and faster. She scares me. Finally, Mother stops at the door and is silent. She looks at me for a while and then motions to me to join her. I feel that something bad is about to happen.

She says to me in a low and serious voice, "You are ten years old. You are still strong. You must do this. You have to go and find some food."

As she pushes me out the door, she continues. "You must find some food. If Pista and Katika don't get something to eat soon, they will die. If you do not find any food, do not bother to come back."

I want to protest. I want to beg to stay, but I don't. I feel her eyes on me as I walk away, and then I hear the door close. Outside it is quiet. There have not been too many daytime bombardments lately, nor has the sound of the artillery fire come any closer. I am thinking about my mother's remarks: "Find some food or we will die."

I walk slowly toward the water. Balatonkenese is just a narrow strip of land between the lake and the sandy mountains. It is easy to find your way around. The ditch we almost froze to death in when we arrived in Balatonkenese is right ahead of me. It is no longer frozen. The weather has changed. There are patches of water everywhere, and the wet road, oily from the tanks, is slippery.

An old man is sitting on the edge of the ditch. His back is turned to me. He's looking out over the lake. He seems large, and his body is bent in the way of older people. He is wearing the typical peasant garb of the region. There is a big bundle next to him, holding his possessions, covered with what looks like a horse blanket. There is food on top of that bundle. I see a loaf of bread with only a small piece missing and a whole salami. My mouth is filling with saliva, and I'm making chewing motions without being able to stop. The old peasant takes a large bite of the salami and puts it next to the bread, and reaches for his flask. I make my move. I grab the bread and the salami and run. By the time he notices what has happened, I am at a safe distance, the food tucked in the front of my shirt. I hear him cursing, but I'm already halfway home. To be sure nobody is following me, I turn into the wrong street at first, slow down, and look around. The street behind me is empty. I turn the next corner and I am back at our hiding place.

The food is rationed to last at least two days. Mother feeds Katika with a soft paste she makes by chewing the bread and then putting it into Katika's mouth with her fingers. Nobody's talking; there are only sounds of chewing and swallowing. Pista sinks back on his bed with a deep sigh of satisfaction. After I eat my share and drink some water, I go to sleep.

From then on, I go out almost every day to "secure" food. That's what Mother calls it—"secure" food. After a few more times, I get lucky and find a better way to get provisions than snatching bread out of the hands of refugees. I discover the location of the kitchen for the German soldiers who are quartered in Balatonkenese. It is a small, undamaged building attached to a larger building that was once the school, now pockmarked by artillery fire. It serves as the local headquarters of the German Army. There is a guard in front, but nobody stops me when I sneak to the back. The small door on the side of the building is well hidden from the street and is used to dispose of garbage from the kitchen. This turns out to be a treasure trove. The very first day I discover that door, I come home with a large loaf of moldy bread. Mother carefully scrapes it and we eat it with pieces of cheese crust I found in the garbage.

I spend a lot of time hanging out around that back door. The German soldiers who are the cooks working in the kitchen notice me after a while, but they seem friendly and do not send me away. And the quality of the garbage is getting better. Sometimes they leave a package, wrapped in old newspaper, on the side of the dirty piles of garbage. It is meant for me to take and usually contains leftovers—cooked potatoes, onions, and even some meat! One day a soldier opens the door while I am sorting through the garbage, smiles at me, shows me a package in his hands, and then throws it directly at me. I catch it. It turns out to be a large ham bone with most of the meat still on it. That night, after we eat, Mother remarks that even her father, who is an observant Jew, would forgive us for eating non-kosher ham in order to stay alive. I smile to myself remembering all of the ham sandwiches Béla bácsi and I secretly ate together.

I now go out every day to pick up what the soldiers leave for me. Mother keeps on asking me questions.

"Did they ask you your name?"

"No," I say.

"Do they want to see your papers?"

"No," I say.

"Do they want to know whom the food is for?"

"No, Mother," I say, annoyed. "They don't ask me anything. They don't bother me. They never come outside when I am there. And they have never spoken to me. Now please, don't ask me those same questions again and again," I continue angrily.

"Don't get fresh," she says, but I have a good mind to pick a fight with her. Pista comes to my defense. Obviously, he is getting better from all the good food.

"I think by now every German soldier knows that the war is lost," he says. "Maybe they just want to redeem their souls by giving a hungry child some food. I don't think that anybody is going to ask us for our papers again. I did not see any patrols when I went outside this morning."

As I leave that day, I'm curious what food the soldiers will have left for me. Lately, there have been larger portions of cooked meals: meatloaf, stew, potatoes and cabbage, bread and cheese, and one time a large, well-wrapped piece of apple strudel. But when I approach the building, I have a feeling that something is wrong. There is no guard in front and the kitchen window is dark. I check the corner where they usually leave the food, but there is nothing there. The German soldiers have left.

I hear the planes when I'm halfway to our hiding place and I start to run. Mother is at the door shouting, "Quick, quick, get under the table." Pista and Katika are already squeezed in the small space under the table. They are flat on their stomachs. The first bomb hits just as Mother climbs on top of us. The sound of the explosion is deafening and it shakes the already damaged porch. It feels like it is breaking apart and falling down. Big pieces of ceiling are coming loose and debris is gathering around us. Glass and fragments from nearby buildings fly through the oilcloth-covered broken windows. We do not dare to move. Several explosions follow, but none is as close as the first. The planes are moving away.

When we crawl out from under the table, Mother is agitated.

"We cannot stay here," she says. "We will not survive the bombings until the Russians finally reoccupy the village." Mother pulls out our small suitcase and starts to pack whatever we have, including the food. "We are going to go up the mountain," she says. She has heard that there are caves up there called the Turkish Caves. They were used as prisons during the occupation of Hungary by the Turks during the sixteenth century. "The trail is way too narrow for the tanks," explains Mother, "and there's nothing worth bombing up there. We will just have to stay there until the battle is over."

But for now, it's not over, and the battle is raging. The planes come back two more times and there are many explosions but none are as close as the first. We go under the table every time the droning sounds alert us to their coming. When finally it is quiet, it is too late to leave. It is getting dark.

"We will go in the morning," says Mother, "as soon as it is light." Pista is worried. "Are you sure we should do this?" he asks. "Yes," she says, "or do you have a better suggestion?" Pista does not answer. "We have to ration the little food we still have," she adds. "We don't know how long we will have to spend on the mountain."

We leave at dawn, but it is not early enough. All of the villagers are on their feet climbing up the mountain. The narrow path, uneven and overgrown, is almost blocked with people, mostly women whose men are away at war, children, and old people, some of whom are barely able to walk.

Mother whispers something to Pista, who is carrying the suitcase, then turns to me and puts Katika in my arms. "You can carry Katika, you are strong," she says. "Stay with Pista. I am going ahead. I want to make sure we have room in one of the caves close to the top of the mountain. You do not have to hurry. I will wait for you there." And she is gone. I see her for a few minutes, making her way through groups of people. It is embarrassing the way she pushes through the crowd to get ahead. I am glad I am not with her. I see her for a while until she disappears behind a curve.

Soon, there are few trees to hold on to and the path is steeper and increasingly narrow. It is dangerous. It is becoming more and more difficult to climb as we get closer to the top. We advance very slowly and stop several times. Katika is very light for a two-year-old but she becomes heavier as the climb goes on. Only a few people are climbing as high as we are. Some have stopped at lower caves or just walked into the woods to hide. I don't think I can take another step. Katika is hanging on to my neck and Pista is holding me and pushing me from the back, when I hear, "Pista." It's my mother's voice, and then again, "Pista," Suddenly, we are at the entrance to the cave she has found.

"There are people here already," she says, "but there is still room for us." She takes Katika from me and I fall to the ground. She pulls me up and says, "There is no time for that." I hear the planes. "Let's get inside."

The day's first wave of bombardments is just about to begin.

Our place in the cave is the back corner on the left. As the droning sound of the planes comes closer, more people arrive, demanding to share the space until we are packed so tight that I can't move when I am lying down. I stay in that position and get up only when the wave of planes flies past. There is little reprieve until the next bombers arrive.

Our food supply is running out. Yesterday was the last time we ate any food. The little salami and bread we brought in the brown suitcase is gone, and so is the food of all the other people. My stomach really hurts. The pain is going to spread. I know it will slowly move into my arms and legs. When it reaches my head, I am in trouble. I start to act silly, jumping around and saying, "Can I go to Susie's house? Her mother always serves cakes." I am so hungry. Mother keeps saying, "Two more days inside this cave and we will die." Pista's diarrhea is back and sometimes he doesn't make it outside because of the planes. The people in the cave made a little space that we use as a toilet when we can't get outside. And Katika is mute.

A defector from the Hungarian Army arrives at the cave, and someone invites him to come in. He could hide among us, but he declines, saying that he will go into the woods. He offers to leave his big bag, and I see him give it to one of the older women sitting near the entrance. When she opens the bag, she cries out, "Oh, dear Jesus." The sack is full of fresh eggs, some broken, which the soldier collected from the empty farmhouses in the village. "What are we going to do with all these raw eggs?" somebody asks. Another old peasant woman in the cave speaks up, "I have some sugar." The two women mix up a delicious paste of sugar and egg in a bowl. They decide to share it with everybody in the cave. A spoon goes around from mouth to mouth. I eat the egg and sugar from the spoon. It tastes amazing, and I want more. The old woman says, "Don't worry. There is enough for the spoon to go around tomorrow." But we are a lot of hungry people in this cave. I worry.

I cannot stand having so many people around me. At the next pause between the waves of bomber planes, I work my way forward, crawling and stepping over small children or sleeping people and the old who cannot move. At the entrance, I stand up and stretch and look out over the beautiful lake. It is a clear and sunny day, and the water is very still. Soon, I notice two fighter planes much smaller and more graceful than the bombers that they usually accompany. The bigger one is a Russian plane, and the other, the German, is flying just under it. They look like large birds chasing each other, flying in circles up and down and around and having fun. I think how lovely they are to watch until I realize what they are really doing. They are actually chasing each other to kill. "Look," I cry. "It's a dogfight." Nobody in the cave is particularly interested, except an old man who yells back, "Tell us what's going on, kid."

"They are fighting," I say. "They are trying to position themselves so that one is on top of the other to shoot down the one below." I cannot take my eyes off them. I still think they are beautiful. "They dance," I tell the people in the cave. "They tango," I say.

Then suddenly, there is a flash of light from the plane above. I shudder when I see flames shoot out of the lower plane as it breaks apart.

"The German plane is hit," I shout. I am still standing at the entrance but with my back to the lake because I can no longer look. I begin to go back into the cave when somebody asks me, "Has the pilot jumped out?"

Looking back, I see the damaged plane broken in half, both parts burning and spiraling in large circles around and around toward the water. I see a parachute as well with a person attached slowly descending. Suddenly, I hear a shot and the parachute collapses, and both parachute and pilot plummet toward the lake. Fast, I think—too, too fast.

The Russian plane, having finished its business destroying the German plane and shooting the parachute and the pilot down, is advancing toward our hill. The plane is only at a slightly higher altitude than the mouth of our cave. I can see the machine gun, and I can see the pilot take aim.

"Kid!" I hear the old man yell. "Come in!"

But it is too late. I hear the bullet hit the wall on my left and another stirring up the dust between my feet, a lot of dust. I can barely see, but I hear my mother screaming.

"You stupid girl!" she yells and pulls me back into the safety of the cave. "You will stay here in this corner in the back of the cave until this is over." I do as she says, but I can hardly bear it.

People are surrounding me and crowding me. There is no room. There is no room at all, and I feel I cannot breathe. What I would like to do is to scream and push them all away, but that is not possible. Instead, I think of my Grandmother Adél, whom

I love. I decide to go elsewhere to visit with her. "My sweet Erika," she says, "don't be upset. This will be over soon, and you will be back in your lovely yellow room and you won't have to share it with anyone." I can feel her hands stroking my hair. "My little one," she says, "go to sleep now." And I do.

Voices wake me up. There is excited talk around me. Another Hungarian defector is in the cave. He wants to hide and says, "The Russians have taken the village, and the whole area around it. The front line now is farther west, closer to the Austrian border. I will not stay here. It could be dangerous for you. I will go find the other defectors in the woods." After he leaves, everybody in the cave is talking about whether to go back to the village or stay a little while longer until things in the area are safe. They want to protect their houses from being plundered or occupied by Russian soldiers or officers, but they don't want to be killed. Probably they are dreaming of their hidden food supplies. Mother decides that we will leave the next morning. We all go to sleep.

Bright and early in the day, we are on our way back to the village. The path coming up the mountain seemed steep but going back down seems even more treacherous. Mother's burned wrist is acting up. She says, "This damned thing hurts." The newspaper wrapped around her wound has long shredded. "I don't dare to take it off completely," she says. "It is sticking." It is hard for her to carry Katika. I carry her most of the way down, but the pebbles and wet leaves, some of them still frozen from the earlier cold spell, make it difficult and slippery. As we approach the house with the veranda that had been our home for the past couple of weeks before we headed to the mountains, Pista says, "I don't see it. I don't think that our place is here anymore."

"Are you sure?" Mother asks. "It is just over there."

Pista is adamant. "No," he says, "you see the porch of the next house. Ours is destroyed."

"Then we will go to the other porch," says Mother. Nobody stops us. There are a few people there already. Some are sitting on blankets. Some are just standing around. This porch is big and in the far corner there is a piano. I can't believe that this beautiful black piano is there in the back corner of the porch. The roof of the porch is damaged and will probably leak with the first spring rain. Mother points to the roof and says, "Let's take the place under the piano." Pista plays a few notes. Then he goes to the ruin of our former porch. He comes back with a couple of blankets and two undamaged pillows. We settle down. Katika is very quiet.

Some of the other people on the porch tell us that the rooms of the house are occupied by Russian officers. "But they are not bad," they say. "The soldiers are quite nice, and occasionally they even let us use the bathroom inside the house." Mother says how nice that is, but that is not the worry right now. We are desperately hungry. She says, "Shall we try to buy something? There are no stores, but maybe we can find some local people who would sell us a loaf of bread or whatever they have." I know we have money, and I also know where Mother keeps it. She had sewn a pocket into her garter belt that she wears constantly although she doesn't have any stockings. Pista doesn't think she should go out because of the soldiers. He is going to go into the village to try to buy food. Mother agrees and goes to the bathroom to get some of the hidden money out of her garter belt.

CHAPTER NINE

BALATONKENESE

• Spring 1945 •

I T TAKES PISTA A while to come back. He is carrying a large loaf of peasant bread, clutching it to his chest like a baby. I can smell it from where I sit under the piano, and it smells so good. I think I could eat that whole bread by myself. Mother takes out our only knife from the little brown suitcase and hands it to Pista to slice the bread.

A man, his wife, and his son are sitting on the other side of the porch. When he sees Pista with the bread, he gets up slowly and approaches. "Can I buy some bread from you?" he asks. Pista's answer is fast and angry. "No," he says and turns away. The man, trembling, grabs Pista's arm. He says something to him that I cannot hear. "No!" shouts Pista, his anger rising. "I said no!" The man answers with loud words that I'm not supposed to understand and hits Pista's chest with his fist. Pista drops the bread; I can see the knife in his raised hand. I am so scared I feel pee trickling down my legs. My mother jumps up and shouts at Pista. "Stop, Pista, stop! No, no, no." The man's wife comes running up to them too, pulling her husband away. Mother takes the knife from Pista, who is shaking, and picks up the bread from the floor. Not taking her eyes from Pista, she starts to slice.

Pista sits down, leaning against a leg of the piano. He looks dejected; he is hunched over shaking and not looking at anyone. Mother has trouble slicing the bread; it is so fresh it is hard to cut. She decides to tear it into chunks. She gives me one to share with Katika, and she brings another to Pista, whispering, "This is for the man over there, and his wife and his son. I think you should bring it over to them. We have enough for now and we will find some more tomorrow." Pista looks up and I can see that he is crying. He gets up and without a sound, takes the bread and walks over to the other side of the porch. Before Pista even gets close, I hear the man say, "I am so sorry." I see the man's wife starting to cry. Mother looks relieved that the tension seems to have lifted, but she whispers to me, "Pista has changed since he escaped from the front. I'm scared that one day he may get into serious trouble. He is severely shell-shocked." I too am upset. I have never seen Pista this angry and cruel before. He has always been polite. He seems like a stranger to me. I am frightened by the change.

I go to the bathroom to clean up. When I come back, Pista is still sitting and talking to that family while they eat their bread. Some other people on the porch come up to Mother to say how glad they are that the fight was averted. A young woman named Susan stays with us under the piano for a while, munching on a piece of bread Mother has given her. I watch her eat. Mother and Pista had been talking about her before. Mother thought she is a beautiful woman. She also suspects that Susan is Jewish.

Now, sitting with us, Susan tells her story. She is Jewish. She is married, has two small children, and is in hiding alone. Her Christian husband, who is in a prominent position at the university, had to officially abandon her or he would have lost his position, his possessions, and even his freedom. Their two children were taken in by his Christian parents, who own a large farm nearby. They are safe with the grandparents because they have fake documents attesting to their pure Christian parentage and are considered to be Aryan. It would have been too dangerous for her in-laws to hide Susan as well, so she has been hiding with her set of fake papers in Balatonkenese. For the last few months, she had been living alone in a rented room in a house nearby; the owners of the house were living in Budapest. She, too, hid in the caves when the serious bombardments started. When she came back to the village, she found a pile of stones and rubbish where her house had been. It had been bombed out, burnt, and plundered. She couldn't even salvage any clothing or a blanket.

I am hungry. Our bread is gone. Pista and Mr. Breuer, the man he had threatened with the knife, are going to the village together to try to buy food. They have become friends over time. They spend most of their days discussing the war and speculating on what will happen afterward. Who will be the new rulers? Who, if anyone, will be brought to justice?

"We will have more information," says Pista, "as soon as we get back to Budapest."

There is some commotion at the entrance to the porch. A couple returning from an attempted trip to the village tell of the dangers. The woman says, "The Russians are taking every able-bodied person with them, putting them to work digging graves, collecting dead bodies, clearing the roads of debris, and having them work in their headquarters cleaning and cooking. We also heard some rumors that women, in particular, should be very careful not to be seen by the soldiers. They might be abducted and not come back. In the end," she said, "we never made it to the village. We were too afraid."

"Here on the porch of this house," says Mother, "not too much harm can come to us, because the building is occupied by Russian officers, not by soldiers. They come and go through this porch all the time. Certainly, other soldiers would not dare to come in here to harm us." Then she turns to Susan, who is sitting with us all the time now, and says, "Have you noticed that good-looking young officer who is coming through the porch more often than all of the others? He is looking at you all the time. Do you think maybe he is flirting with you?" Susan turns red in the face and admits, "I noticed. I noticed how handsome he is, too. And he is always so clean. I don't even want to get up to try to talk to him. I feel so dirty and ugly."

I can tell when my mother is planning something. I do not know exactly what it is, but she is going around talking to the two other women she has befriended, and then she comes back to Susan. Mostly they whisper, and I don't hear what they are saying. Mother comes to me and asks me to show her my undershirt. I know not to say no to my mother. So I open my blouse and show her the dirty undershirt I have worn for a long time. She takes a look and says, "It will do fine when I wash it. Take it off." She is already carrying a few garments that she got from some of the other women. She disappears into the bathroom, the one we are allowed to use. Mother comes back with a freshly washed and dripping heap of clothing. She improvises spaces to hang them to dry on the bottom of the piano, from the edges of the piano, on some pieces of wood she lays across our little suitcase, or wherever they can dry in the air.

Pista is angry with her. "What the hell are you doing? And if it is what I think it is, do you realize how dangerous it could be?!" I am also angry. I don't have an undershirt, and due to my budding breasts, my blouse keeps popping open. "When can I have my undershirt back? And why did you take it, anyway?" But there is no answer for any of our questions.

The next morning, all of the now dry and clean clothes have

disappeared from where they were hanging. Susan and Mother go into the bathroom together. They do not come back for quite a while. When they return, Susan's hair is combed and looks nice and shiny. She is smiling. Soon, the young officer passes by as usual. This time, Susan returns his smile with her own and goes up to him, saying in Hungarian, "I welcome you to Hungary." With an astonished look on his face, the officer replies in Russian. I don't understand what he says, but I know that it is friendly.

The officer's arm is now around Susan's waist, and he slowly escorts her into the house. There are some whispers from the ladies and some astonished sounds from all. I really don't know what is going on. Mother says in a somewhat triumphant whisper, "We won't be hungry much longer."

Susan is gone for the whole day and the whole night. When she returns the following morning, she brings loaves of bread, cheese, ham, salami, and milk. It is so much food that she can hardly carry it all. By this time, most everybody realizes what has happened and greets her with cheers, hurrahs, and hugs, especially when she goes back into the house and comes out again carrying a large pot of steaming coffee and mugs. It seems that the food supply for our little group is secure as long as we stay on the porch and Susan stays with the officer.

After a few days of eating good food and drinking milk, Katika starts to come back to life. She is talking and getting up by herself to walk. Best of all, she asks to go to the bathroom again. I spend my time with her playing and trying to teach her new things. Now that she is better, she doesn't want to leave my side. I usually walk around the porch with Katika next to me or in my arms.

Everybody is talking about the end of the war and whether Budapest has yet been liberated. How many people were killed during the bombardments? What happened to the ghetto? Mother is getting very worried. She wants to know if her parents survived the ghetto. She wants to find out who of our family survived and who did not. I think about my cousins, Marika and Tom, and hope they are okay. But there is no way to communicate with anybody in the city. We have no phones, no electricity, no anything, so there's no way to get in touch.

We've been eating and getting stronger for a while. Everyone in our little group is feeling better, but we are getting restless. I notice Susan is not smiling as much since she found out that her captain will soon have to leave, although she is still cheerful. Whenever he is on duty, she comes to sit with us and speaks about how much she misses her children and how she would love to see them. Pista wants information about whether the war is definitely over. Have the Germans surrendered and have they been totally defeated? We know very little of what is going on outside of our porch.

One day, Susan starts to talk about her in-laws' farm. She says, "If I weren't so afraid, I would like to go there. I know the roads, but as a woman alone, there is no way that I can undertake this journey." She continues, "I can't stay here. I have to find out what happened to my children, but I can't risk trying to get there by myself." She looks at Mother and says, "It's only about twenty kilometers away. It's a big farm. Would you all like to accompany me? Do you think you can walk that far?" Mother looks to Pista. He says, "Yes. I definitely think we can go. I think we can walk if we don't move too fast."

Susan is delighted. "My captain leaves tonight. Let's all go tomorrow," she says. "I will get food to take with us. We should leave as early in the morning as possible so that we get there in daylight."

CHAPTER TEN

THE FARM

• 1945 •

THE TREK TO THE farm turns out to be more difficult than Susan anticipated. The main roads are occupied by tanks and other army vehicles, and the debris of the battle has not been completely cleared away. We stay on the main road for a while. Susan knows the area very well and leads us toward some back roads that go to her in-laws' farm. Those roads are muddy and still covered with patches of frozen water and leaves left over from the severe winter, and the mud and ice reaches up to my bare ankles. The newspaper wrapped around my shoes and fastened with some twine stops protecting my feet. Water and muddy ice slip into the holes through the soles of my shoes.

Most of these roads are quite deserted without too many people. There are only a few stationary tanks and small army vehicles and other signs of the Russian Army's presence. Somehow, we are more frightened on the back roads than we were marching alongside the moving tanks and soldiers on the main road. "Let's cut across these fields," Susan says. "We'll get back to the main roads faster. It could be a much shorter trip." Pista says, "No way. Many of these fields are mined." So we go back to the main road on a path the long way around and continue walking with the tanks on one side of us and all kinds of debris on the other.

"It seems like most of the dead bodies have been cleared away," says Mother. "We haven't seen any this time like on the trip to Balatonkenese." But we don't talk very much now. We concentrate on walking. We all take turns carrying Katika. Susan walks well, but the rest of us do not. We have not moved much under the piano. My legs feel stiff, and they don't go where I want them to go. My knees buckle, especially when I carry Katika. When it is Pista's turn to pick her up, he is too weak and almost falls. Mother takes Katika instead and says, "Our friends, the Breuers, were right. This trip may be almost more than we can handle."

But we keep walking as best as we can. It is dusk. We have been walking for about seven hours. Suddenly, Susan screams, "We are almost there. I see that house over there—it is not the farm, but I know it. We can't see our place yet, but it is only about a kilometer away. I hope it is still here. I hope it hasn't been hit. I hope my children are alive, and I hope that they rec-ognize me." She is very nervous. She is trembling, shaking, cry-ing. She starts walking faster and faster—we cannot keep up with her. "Forgive me," she says. "I have to go ahead, but you can't miss the farm. Just stay on the main road. It's on the left."

I don't think I can go much farther. My feet are frozen. My legs are buckling under me, and I am just too tired to continue. It is getting dark, and I think this is the end of the road for me. But then I look up, and I see it. I yell, "I see it. I see it. That is the farm over there. There is a huge yard on the side of it. It must be the farm." We go a little faster. We have new energy now that we can see where we are going. As we are crossing the yard toward the door of the house, we see Susan and her two children on the porch waiting for us. There are hugs and greetings, and we are escorted into a big kitchen. Everything here seems to be big. The kitchen has a big fireplace in it, which also serves as the stove. On either side of it are big upholstered benches with blankets. In the center of the room is a large, long table with a bench on one side and chairs on the other. I wonder how many other people live here. Susan's in-laws are both standing in the kitchen waiting for us and greet us politely. There is food on the table and we are shown the bathroom to clean up before we sit down to eat. I am trying to remember when we last sat down at a table to eat on plates with forks and knives. We are also shown a room where Mother and Pista will sleep. The benches on either side of the fireplace are for Katika and me. By the time we eat, we are too tired to enjoy it. At least I can hardly wait to lie down on that bench and go to sleep.

The next morning, there is milk and homemade bread for breakfast. Mother and Pista are busy talking to Susan. After breakfast, Katika and I go outside to explore. There is a large well in the middle of the yard. Katika wants to look inside the well so I lift her up to show her the bucket hanging on the chain and how to lift and lower it with the crank. A horse-drawn wagon is coming into the yard and slowly moves around the well. A young-looking peasant in a flowing white shirt and embroidered vest is the driver. Both Katika and I are watching him. He greets us with a friendly hello and continues on his way toward the path on the far end of the yard. I notice that the wagon is loaded with potatoes and cabbages and other provisions. We walk around the yard some more and see other peasants, not all of them dressed as nicely as the first. They are milling about, carrying buckets, going on the back path, and leading a horse to the trough at the back of the yard to drink. Katika and I walk back to the house.

The in-laws, Susan, Pista, and Mother are sitting around the kitchen table. It looks like there is a serious conversation going on. Mother says, "Please stay outside for a little longer." She's extremely serious, and I am frightened. I want to know what they are planning.

When we are finally allowed back into the kitchen, we are invited to sit at the table as well. Katika is sitting on Mother's lap while we are talking. She's young, but she knows when to keep quiet.

"You know how important it is to find out if your grandparents are alive," Mother says, "and who else from the family survived. We decided, now that we know that Budapest too has been liberated, to get back to Budapest as fast as we can. Of course, there are no trains running as yet, so we will have to walk or get a ride. Susan's in-laws," she continues, "have agreed to keep you here until we get back." She is looking at me all the while she says this, but I don't know what to say. I am so frightened. My stomach feels like a knotted rag and my tongue for reasons unknown is stuck to the roof of my mouth. Am I supposed to say something? Am I allowed to tell them how scared I am? Am I allowed to protest? Can I tell them that I am not yet eleven years old and don't want to take care of Katika all by myself? "When will you come back?" I manage to ask after a while. "We are going to be back as fast as possible," says Mother with a sigh. I can tell there is no way that she will change her mind.

I am trying very hard not to cry, but I cannot stop it. Mother is looking at me. She is saying, "Don't cry. You can do it. Thank god, Katika is better, and you will take good care of her as if you were her mother." I am still crying. Susan comes to my rescue and says, "Don't worry. I am here too. You can always come to me and have Katika play with my children. You will see. We will be okay, and they will be back sooner than you think." The next day they are gone.

Katika and I spend most of our time sitting on one of the stones, tree trunks, and other things in the big yard watching the peasants carry on with their business. The weather has turned quite nice, and both Katika and I are cleaned up and wearing some donated clothes. We both have had a bath in a big pewter tub located in the back of the kitchen.

Soon after Mother and Pista leave, I notice that as much as I want to help in the kitchen, my help is not welcome. Susan's in-laws are avoiding Katika and me. I somehow have the feeling they would be much happier if we were not around. When some neighbors visit one afternoon, we are in the kitchen but are told to go outside. We are not introduced but hear them speaking about us as if we are not there. "They are children of Susan's friends from the city, and she is doing them a favor while they go to Budapest." As we are leaving the kitchen, Susan is just on the way in, and she says to me in a low voice, "Those neighbors are not good people. It is better if you do not come in, and don't answer any questions should they ask you anything as they are leaving."

I'm feeling more and more uncomfortable, not knowing what I'm supposed to do or not do. I am missing my mother. Katika, too, is upset. "I don't like them," she says in her loud child's voice. "Be quiet," I say. "Don't say that. We are not supposed to upset those people."

We stay in the yard a lot each day. It is really the only place where we spend our time. Actually, we spend our time in the far corner of the yard, which Susan's mother-in-law pointed out as the place where we are allowed to stay. Sometimes Susan is with us as are her two children, who play with Katika.

Once, the mother-in-law visits our corner and addresses Susan's children. "I have some treats for you. You have to come into the house to get them." She doesn't say anything to us or to Susan, but I notice the look she gives her that means *You better come in too. I don't want you around those Jewish kids.*

I am becoming really upset. I don't know how long Mother and Pista have been gone, but it is a long time, maybe a week or maybe more. I wonder if they are dead. I feel like an orphan. If they were not dead, I think they should have been back already. How can they leave us alone for so long? And mostly, how can they leave us with all these Jew-hating people? Don't they know how bad it is here for Katika and me? How Susan's in-laws try to make us invisible? Hungarian peasants seem to be anti-Semites by birth, and Susan's in-laws are afraid that somebody might find out that their grandchildren are Jewish.

To pass the time of day, I count all the wagons coming into the yard every morning. They are usually driven by young farmhands. By now, I am quite familiar with the daily activities of the farm. I sit on my stone, Katika next to me, and watch. This morning, though, something is not quite right. The wagon coming through the entrance is drawn by a horse that doesn't look as well fed or as well kept as the ones belonging to the farm. Instead of a peasant boy holding the reins, there are two people sitting on the bench. I look and look again. I can't believe it. I don't believe it. It cannot be true. Mother and Pista are driving the wagon! I jump up. I am totally beside myself. I start to scream. I don't want to feel this way, but I cannot help myself. I run toward the wagon screaming, "Mother. Mother! You're here! You're not dead!" I try to climb up on the wagon but fall down, and the carriage drags me. I am being dragged and I am holding on. Dust is hitting my face. I don't want to let go. I am pulled

along for a while until Pista manages to stop the horse, but I am
still screaming, "Mother! Mother! You are not dead!"

When Mother gets off the wagon, she says, "I hope you are
not hurt." And then, "Stop crying." Then she picks up Katika.
Everybody from the farm is around us by now, the in-laws and
Susan too. We go inside to have some lunch. Everyone is curious. How did they get to Budapest? There were no trains. But
they were lucky, they tell us. Soon after they left the farm on
foot, they were picked up by a Russian tank driven by two very
tired soldiers who wanted company. Mother sat in the front seat
with the driver while Pista sat in the back, convinced that she
was going to get raped and they would be killed. But nothing
like that happened. The battle-weary Russian driver kept on
talking to Mother in Russian, and Mother, realizing that she was
supposed to keep him awake, kept on talking to him in Hungarian. The way Mother told the story, they had a wonderful
conversation.

The tank drove them all the way to Budapest and dropped
them near our apartment. The three families who were now
living in the apartment would not let them in. Mother and Pista
went to my father's apartment nearby, which was undamaged.
They cleaned up and stayed for a little while, but Father and his
wife already had his sister-in-law, nephew, and niece living with
them in the one-bedroom apartment, so they could not remain
there. Mother and Pista spent the night in a bombed-out grocery store where we used to buy our supplies. The owner of the
store, which had neither doors nor windows, is my mother's
friend. They slept on the floor with some blankets my father had
given them.

In the morning, they went looking for my grandparents in
the ghetto, but neither my grandfather nor my grandmother was

found. It was well-known that the Germans used the ghetto as target practice for their cannons. Mother and Pista were told by neighbors that Grandmother Adél had been wounded by German cannon fire way before the Russians began attacking the city. Many were injured and were taken to various hospitals. They took Grandmother Adél but nobody knew which hospital she was in. Mother learned that Béla bácsi, who was not injured, went out every day looking for her until he was not seen again. His body was found on the sidewalk a day after liberation, a moldy half-chicken in his briefcase that he had been saving for his wife. He was not wounded; he died of hunger.

There were no phones or streetcars in the city. Mother and Pista had to go from hospital to hospital looking for Grandmother Adéle. They finally found her. "Grandma has over two hundred pieces of shrapnel lodged in her legs," Mother tells us. "She is not well, but at least she is in a hospital being cared for and fed."

I am surprised to hear the story from my mother. She does not usually speak about sad things. I watch Pista put his arms around her. I know the sadness she is feeling. I too am very sad. I would like her to come and hug me, but that won't happen. I think of Béla bácsi and how much I will miss him, but I do not cry. Mother would not approve. Everyone in the room is affected by the story. Even Susan's in-laws seem moved. It is silent for a while. Nobody speaks until Mother says in a determined voice, "It's time to think of getting back to Budapest for good."

Mother wants to leave soon, but first, she says, "We need to get some supplies." I'm wondering if we have enough money to buy all the food she wants to take with us. It must be more than the money she has hidden in her garter belt. I think that money was already spent paying Susan's in-laws for keeping Katika and me while they were gone. Obviously, they must have gotten some money in Budapest to buy the buggy and the horse and the food that they are going to buy. We are going to get onions, potatoes, cabbage, smoked meat, and even some sausage from the in-laws' farm. Everybody agrees that you can't put all of this food openly into the carriage because the Russians on the road will stop you and confiscate the provisions. You're lucky if they don't kill you for them. So the carriage is first loaded with lots and lots of hay, the food is hidden, and another layer of hay is placed on top. I find it a lot fun to sit on the hay when we are finally ready to leave. I sit with Katika and play games.

When we say goodbye, I feel that the in-laws are happy to see us go, but Susan is sad. "I will come back to Budapest," she tells us, "as soon as I hear from my husband." The last she knew about him was that he was on the front fighting the Russians with the Hungarian Army. Susan looks very sad and upset. Even though she will be with her in-laws and children, I think to myself that she will be lonely without us, and she must have realized by now that her in-laws don't like Jews.

I'm looking forward to Budapest. I'm going to see my father again. What else am I going to find? My grandfather is dead, my grandmother is in the hospital, and we don't know if my cousins are still alive. We don't have an apartment. The war is over but everything is going to be different.

My family on my mother's side. Back row, left to right: her brother-in-law, Laci bácsi (Auschwitz); her sister, Erzsi néni (Auschwitz); her brother, Pista (Auschwitz survivor); my mother; and my stepfather, Pista. Front row: cousin Marika (Auschwitz); Grandmother Adél néni; me; cousin Jutka; Grandfather Béla bácsi; cousin Tom (Auschwitz); sister-in-law Klari néni; and baby Gyuri.

My family on my father's side. Back row: my father, Henry; my mother; Paly (half brother to my father, killed in a camp); Aunt Hedi; and Richard, my father's brother. Front row: Kato néni and her husband, Ignác.

Wedding picture of my mother and father at the famous Dohány Utcai Synagogue, 1932.

Grandmother Adél néni, 1937.

Grandfather Béla bácsi.

Mother and me. I am six months old.

Father and me. Budapest, 1942.

Mother's husband Pista, Katika, my mother, and me. Budapest, 1948.

My mentor and best friend at the convent in St. Pölten, Mother Shushinsky, 1950.

A class picture at St. Joseph's convent in London, 1950.

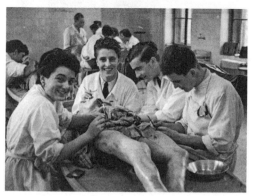

Medical school, University of Vienna, 1954.

The "hiding place" in Kisláng where we were from 1943–44. Picture taken in 2010, on a visit with my grandchildren.

The attic in Kisláng, where we hid Pista October 15, 1944–January 5, 1945. Picture taken 2010.

The mountainside and the caves in Balatonkenese, 1945. Photos taken in 1993.

My daughter, Marion, in the cave on the occasion of our "roots trip," 1993.

Israeli trip with my mother and Pista at a reception with David Ben-Gurion, front row, center (myself and my then-husband to either side of Ben-Gurion, and my mother in a floral shirt and Pista in sunglasses on the far right).

My first husband, Tom, chairing a philanthropic dinner with Saidye and Charles Bronfman, late 1980.

Dinner with Prime Minister Pierre Trudeau; my first husband, Tom, and my son, Robert, saying hello! Mid-1980s.

Me, my mother, and Katika at our mother's nursing home.

Mother and her caretaker Helen, 1996.

Mother and me, 1997.

Mother's tombstone, added to her parents', in a Budapest Jewish cemetery.

BOOK TWO

"We have to do everything necessary so that we can get back to normal life."

CHAPTER ELEVEN

BUDAPEST

• 1945 •

APPROACHING BUDAPEST IN OUR horse-drawn carriage, we are tired and covered in hay. We encounter very little danger on the trip. The roads are quiet. We expect Russian soldiers, tanks, or military equipment, but we do not encounter any. Most of the traffic consists of carriages like our own. People are trying to get home in both directions. As we pull into the city, the first things I notice are the bomb-damaged houses showing the imprint of the heavy fighting in and around the city. A lot of the debris from the damaged buildings is still uncollected, clogging some of the streets. Even though the city is quiet, it looks like a battlefield.

There are few people on the streets, only military patrols. The stores are closed, most store windows are broken, and some are barred with wooden planks or metal blinds. There are no lights on the streets, and all the beautiful, familiar places where we lived and went about our lives look different and strange.

Mother tells me that she spoke to my father before she and Pista came to pick us up at the farm. "He said he would love you to stay with him and Anni néni for a while. You like Anni néni and she likes you. She's always delighted to see you. They are both waiting for you." I am excited about seeing my father again and staying with them, but I don't feel good about leaving Katika and letting all of them go to sleep in the ruined grocery store again.

We park the carriage in the front of the store and lock the gate of the courtyard. We walk over to my father's apartment, bringing him some provisions. When Anni néni opens the door, she gives me a big hug and I can tell she is really happy to see me. Father is standing next to her beaming happily. He hugs me and calls me the apple of his eye, the star in his sky, the brightest sunshine in his day, and a few more of his endearing words. I know them all and right away I feel at home. We sit around for a while, catching up with our stories. Then there is a discussion about the de-licing project offered at some of the hospitals in the city. The next day Mother insists that we go to one of the hospitals for de-licing.

At the disinfecting station, they take away all of our clothes. When Mother removes her dress, the attendant who is in charge of the de-licing tells her to remove the shoulder pads from the dress as well. To our disgust, we discover a hive of lice living under the pads. All of our clothing is taken away and thrown into a disinfectant bath, and they come back smaller and with more holes than before.

While we are naked, we are sprayed with a very ill-smelling liquid and then rinsed off with a hose. We are given a clean towel to dry ourselves, and then proceed, still naked, to another room for the de-licing of our hair, which consists of shaving not only our heads but our entire bodies. Mother is not ready to allow them to do that, and she certainly is not going to let them cut off my hair. My hair is beautiful, and I wear it in two thick pigtails. We agree to take a lice comb and a special liquid with us when we leave to use on our hair. Mother takes on the task of de-licing my hair. After Father walks me every morning to the grocery store, Mother spreads paper on the floor, and I sit on a three-legged stool while she combs and recombs my hair looking for those lice. It is sheer hell. It hurts. I try to tell her to stop, but she won't. This goes on each day until she declares that I am lice-free.

Anni néni is eager to please me. She provides me with some very nice clothes. She asks me about the kind of food I would like to eat, which is something I haven't been asked in a long time. One day I tell her, "Raspberries with whipped cream." She laughs and so does my father, because although it is now May and raspberry season, very few stores are open and none of them sell fresh food. Nobody has heard of cream in a long, long time either, but Anni néni, who is a resourceful woman, says, "I think I will have to make a trip to the country tomorrow."

She does. She finds a way to get to the country with some friends and comes back with a huge bag of raspberries and at least a liter of fresh cream. I have three helpings of berries with whipped cream and later develop the most horrible stomach-ache, but I had enjoyed the dessert a lot.

Father and I visit Mother, Katika, and Pista every day. We listen to their efforts to get our apartment back. Sometimes we take Katika back with us so Pista and Mother can look after their business. Slowly, the authorities are acknowledging the rights of people to their former homes and helping them. I hope we can soon move back into the old apartment. It did not suffer serious damage, although it is very close to several important buildings that were severely affected by the bombardments, like the basilica, some embassies, and the famous Dohány Utcai Synagogue.

One day, Mother, Pista, Father, and Anni néni are sitting in Father's living room discussing how difficult it is to find food in the bombed-out city. Mother and Pista still own the horse and buggy and they decide to go back to Kisláng to pick up food and "some other goodies." Nobody talks about what those goodies are exactly, but I know that there are some treasures buried somewhere in the fields behind Laci bácsi's house. I guess it is money and jewelry. My father cautions that they should be very careful to dig it up only at night when nobody can see them. "Even the main roads are not safe. You don't know who might be killers. Sometimes it is the Russians, sometimes it is desperate Hungarians, sometimes refugees or hungry people," he says. I am frightened when I hear my father say that and ask Mother if they really have to go. She says, "Either we go or we go hungry."

After Anni néni agrees that Katika can move in with us, they leave. They are supposed to be back in two days, but they do not appear then. Everybody is very nervous. Father is pacing up and down. Anni néni is trying to play with Katika. I attempt to read, but nothing works. We are worried sick. Finally, in a few more days, they are back.

They walk in the door after parking the buggy in the court-yard of the grocery store again. They have brought some eggs, flour, bread, all kinds of fruit, and a little suitcase that I assume holds the "goodies," which they carefully put on the table. There are hugs and kisses and happy tears on my part. But they look sad. We have food, we have the goodies, so what is wrong? It seems to me that something is very, very wrong. There is whispered conversation between my father and Pista. Then they both look at me and now I know for sure something bad has happened. Mother comes over to me, looks into my eyes, and says in a low voice, "I wish there was another way to tell you but there isn't. Laci bácsi died in the fields. He stepped on a land mine and died before anybody could help him."

I am not quite sure that I have heard right. "What happened?" I ask her, and she tells me again. Actually, I still don't believe her. I cannot imagine Laci bácsi dead. "Did he not see where he was going?" I ask. But I know as soon as I've said it how stupid that sounds. You don't see land mines lying around in the fields. Nobody is saying anything. The room is silent and so am I. I feel like crying but the tears do not come. I wait to wake up from this bad dream, but I am not asleep. Laci bácsi is dead. He was my friend. He taught me a lot of things and I really loved him.

"How are Janos and Marta and Sara néni?" I ask after a while but nobody answers. Later, Mother, Katika, and Pista leave. Anni néni prepares food but I cannot eat.

SOON, OUR APARTMENT BECOMES available and we move in. We have very little furniture, but my father gives us a few pieces and the furniture in my room is still there. After Mother cleans it all up, we are fairly comfortable. I am glad to be back with her and Pista. Although I loved staying at my father's place, I missed Katika and I worry about her. I know that she missed me a lot too.

We have been attempting to find out about some of our relatives. Mother's brother and his family were taken to a concentration camp. We do not know if they are alive, the same with Mother's sister, Erzsi, and my cousins Tom and Marika. Some people who stayed alive are slowly coming back from the camps and bringing news of others who didn't. That's how we find out that my father's brother-in-law was exterminated. We still don't know where his sister, my Aunt Hedi, and his mother, my grandmother Kato néni, ended up after leaving Kisláng when we did to escape the second German occupation. Mother found out that they went another route, south instead of east within Russian territory, and crossed the Danube and never ended up reoccupied by Germans. But where are they now? My father has not heard from them, but that is not surprising since there is no phone or mail service. He doesn't seem to be too worried so I don't worry either. He says it is difficult for two women alone with children to find safe transportation back to Budapest. He is certain that they will surprise us and arrive soon. "Kato néni," says Father, "will sing her way through anything."

There were not that many relatives of Pista's in Budapest to worry about, except an uncle and a second cousin, who was a musician. The last we had heard of Pista's mother, grandmother, and aunts in Yugoslavia was when Olga néni visited us in Budapest in her nun's habit on her way to Bezdan. Now Pista is trying to find out what happened to Olga néni and the rest of his family. Pista learned from a friend, a lawyer, that his uncle had died in the Budapest ghetto and that he is the sole heir to a sizable fortune, including a bag of diamonds and valuable stocks.

Mother and I visit Grandmother Adél in the hospital. She is very happy to see me and is looking forward to living with us when she gets better. I'm wondering how we will all fit into our little apartment, but there is talk of buying a house. It seems that we can afford it with Pista's inheritance, or at least that is what I hear Mother and Pista discuss. They find a bomb-damaged house in a good neighborhood with a great school nearby, and they buy it and immediately begin renovations. When school starts in the fall, I will go to the new school. It will be the first time in two years that I am back in classes.

Father is moving too. He is giving up the apartment in the

city for a bigger and better apartment in the suburbs. I am worried about the distance between our new house and his new apartment, but he tells me not to worry. He has just bought a motorcycle. I have to keep that a secret from Mother because she would never let me ride with him on a motorcycle. I am very excited, and after my first ride I have a hard time not talking about it, but know that if I do, Mother would never let me visit with him again.

Father is very busy because a lot of people whose businesses he saved during the German occupation have survived, and he is now in the process of returning their properties to them. He also administered some apartment houses on behalf of the owners, and he is giving them back to their rightful owners. Usually, he is well rewarded for his work, but certainly he is not as well to do as he was during the war. To me, it seems that it is a very honorable thing that he is doing, but Mother disagrees.

"How come," she says, "he doesn't keep at least some of the property? After all, without him they would have lost it all."

"You don't understand," I say to Mother. "Father told me that it was agreed upon that whoever survives gets their property back. Also, he said the relatives of those unfortunate people who did not come back alive also have a right to collect their inheritance from him."

Mother is not convinced. "That's typical of your father," she says. "He is a born bohemian. He does not know how to hold on to money. When he has it, he gives it freely, and when he doesn't, he expects you to give it freely to him."

I don't see much wrong with that and end up thinking how lucky we are that my father was a bohemian and saved all our lives. Pista agrees and tells mother never to criticize my father because without his generosity and courage, none of us would be alive. Father himself does not seem to worry about money. "I have enough," he says. "A number of the people who entrusted their fortunes to me unfortunately have not come back, nor have any claims been made on their behalf. As yet, I don't have to worry."

Many people in our immediate family have not come back, like Aunt Erzsi, my mother's sister; her husband, Lanci Laci; and my cousins Marika and Tom. My mother goes to the refugee center and finds their names on the first official list of people gassed in Auschwitz. She also finds the name of Pista's family from Bezdan, including his mother, Olga néni, the nun. Other relatives who have not returned and are not found on the register are confirmed dead by returning friends who survived. The daily conversation among my mother and her friends is all about who is alive and who is dead.

The only good news comes when my grandmother Kato néni and my Aunt Hedi and her two children show up in Budapest. They survived in a little village across the Danube until they too were liberated.

CHAPTER TWELVE

BUDAPEST TO VIENNA

• 1945–1948 •

I T IS THE FIRST day of school. Mother is busy braiding my hair.
She believes that girls of good families who have "normal"
lives should not go to school with thick black hair down to their
shoulders, no matter how clean it is. "It should be neatly braided
and preferably held together at the end with a respectable bow,"
she says. I decide that I will take the bow and braid out as soon
as I leave the house, but I haven't gotten away yet. She wants to
talk to me before I leave.

"Be sure you don't forget that you are a good Christian girl
and behave accordingly."

I find that remark most distressing and try to argue with her
again, as I have done many times before. "The war is over," I say.
"Why do we have to continue lying? I do not want to be a Catholic girl anymore. I want to be a Jewish girl and talk about what
my life was like during the war. I'd like to talk about my cousins
and my aunts and uncles who were all killed in Auschwitz. I want
to talk about how we survived the war. Why don't you want to
talk about anything that happened to us? Grandmother and you
talk about it all of the time."

Questioning my mother is a mistake. Her anger, as usual, is instantaneous and explosive. She screams at me. "I saved your life, disregarding great danger. How dare you refuse my sacrifice? You don't seem to understand. It was for you and it still is for you in the interest of your future. How can you be so selfish, so stupid? I warn you—don't challenge me."

I look to Pista for support. Maybe he can tell her to be reasonable. But he shakes his head and walks away to our new car to drive me to school. We just bought the car. It is a rickety old Fiat he calls Peppy that is falling apart, but it runs. During the drive, I ask him, "Why do we have to continue pretending?" His answer does not help. "No matter what I think, we have to do what your mother says. Without her, we would not have survived."

I go to a school called Baár-Madas, an all-girl school, not too far from the house we are rebuilding. It has been two years since I was in a classroom, as schools were mostly closed during the war. The government decided that in spite of the two-year absence, all students should be admitted to classes appropriate to their age. I'm almost twelve and going to be in the second year of high school.

I arrive early and take a seat near a window looking toward the door, watching the girls come in. I am trying to figure out who else might be Jewish, like me, out of the twenty-eight or thirty girls in my class. Not that it matters, because when Mother registered me at the school, she wrote *Catholic* on the form and requested religious instruction.

As the classroom fills up, the girl who sits down next to me, who has dark curly red hair and a freckled face, says, "I'm Zsuzsa. What's your name?"

"Erika," I say.

"And where do you live?" she asks. When I tell her the address of the house we will soon move to, she lets out a little yelp and says, "That's the street I live on."

I know immediately I am going to like her. I am surprised and delighted to have found a friend so fast. I know instinctively that she is also Jewish and converted. After we move into our new house, I walk to school, rain or shine, with Zsuzsa. One day on the way home, I say, "You're Jewish, aren't you?" She looks at me and says, "How could you miss it? Anybody who looks at my red curly hair and big nose must know that I am Jewish. I have the appearance of a Jewish person, but my family insists on being Protestant."

"Same here," I say. "We are Jewish but pretending to the world that we are Catholic. Do you think that I look Jewish too?"

"Well," she says, "your dark skin and eyes could also be Italian."

"Do your parents' friends know that you are Jewish?" I ask Zsuzsa.

"Sure," she says. "They are mostly converted Jews themselves."

"Just like the friends of my parents," I say. "Aren't they lucky, though? They don't have to go to church like we do."

We laugh about the fact that we may have religious disagreements since I am a Catholic and she is a Protestant. We agree to stay reluctant Christians and keep our secrets.

"Is your family as crazy as mine?" I ask Zsuzsa another time.

"They are crazier," she says. "My father is a tyrant, my mother is a slave driver, and my sister, Sophie, is retarded."

"In my family," I say, "Mother rules everything. You cannot talk to her. She tells my stepfather what to do and if he objects at all, she yells. When she tells you to do something, you better do it. She is not much fun to be around. The only person I get along with," I continue, "is my grandmother Adél, who is living with us. She always takes my side and tries to tell Mother to leave me alone."

Most of the time, though, Zsuzsa and I seem to avoid discussing our families. Instead, we talk about many interesting subjects, like painting, books, and music, and not our impossible home lives.

On our way to school, Zsuzsa and I have to walk through a pretty park by a small chapel. One morning, we go inside to explore. It is lovely. The large stained-glass windows in the nave have fairly dark colors. They represent the Stations of the Cross. The windows lining the sanctuary in a semicircle at the end of the nave are in much lighter colors and depict happier biblical scenes, like the Annunciation, Resurrection, and other joyous events. I find the contrast between the light and the dark, the sorrow and the joy, very impressive, all achieved through the different colors of the stained glass.

Zsuzsa tells me about the summer holiday her family is going to have this year. They are going to Siófok on the shores of Lake Balaton. It is the same lake, but not the same village, where we were in hiding in the caves. Zsuzsa's father likes sailing and owns several small racing boats.

My family decides to spend the summer in Siófok as well, and we rent a large house on the shore. Some of our family friends are there too, but Grandmother Adél is not going with us. She stays in the city with the housekeeper. My other grandmother, Kato néni, who has been happily keeping court in Budapest, is spending the summer nearby in Balatonboglár. My father and his wife are staying with her. I am taking sailing lessons with Zsusza in a small boat with one of her father's crew.

My family spends most of their time on a big boat with friends that has been rented with a crew of two. They go out on the lake almost every day and often go to Badacsony. It is a quaint, small town on a peninsula and is famous for its wine. They come back mostly loud and happy, but other times they are in a fighting mood. Pista and Armin, his business partner in their printing company, seem to get into fights easily. One night at dinner, Mother says to Pista, "Why the hell do you fight with him all the time? You're old friends. You know that he is very worried about money because the printing business is not making much. You know he blames you, Pista. You are the expert in this business, and he doesn't think you are working hard enough to make it a success."

"As it is, I am contributing more than he is," Pista says. "Maybe he is still too shell-shocked." Armin lost his wife and two children in the camps and is newly married to a woman who lost her husband.

The conversation turns, as usual, to talking about those who did not come back. Mother sometimes mentions her sister, Erzsi, who was exterminated. They speak about other acquaintances and friends who didn't come back and cannot participate in the good and "normal" life that the survivors are now living. Sometimes, they stop talking suddenly when they think that the strangers who are walking nearby are not Jews.

I don't understand what exactly is going on with these grown-ups. Are they sad or are they happy? Do they miss the relatives who are dead? They seem so intent on being happy, but I don't think they are. My mother, Pista, and their friends are preoccupied with each other and often do not act very grown up. They lose their tempers very easily. At times I am very uncomfortable around them, especially when they come back from Badacsony, where they have been drinking.

Generally this summer, I prefer to spend my time with my

father and grandmother in Balatonboglár. He is calm and interested in what I am saying and doing and calls me beautiful names. He makes me feel special.

In the fall when we are back at school, Zsuzsa and I have other issues. Neither of us is very athletic. We want to avoid going to gym class, which is obligatory, and try to apply for exemptions. "This is not acceptable," we are informed by our gym teacher, Eva néni, when we present her with doctor's certificates attesting to our inability to perform exercise. "Avoiding gym is going to make you miserable because you will be excluded from all of the other events that my gym classes are going to participate in."

So we stay. Slowly, the classes do take on special meaning beyond athletics. There are field trips, visits to exhibits and sport events, and other organized extracurricular activities in which all students are required to participate. I love the long walks, storytelling, and intimate talks with the older girls who mentor two or three of the younger students at a time.

Eva néni is a small, energetic woman and very curious. She asks questions about our home lives and suggests that we keep a diary to be read in class at a later date. She tells us to write about our parents, their habits, their professions, their friends, and the style we live in. She wants to know if we have a maid or other servants, whether we have any relatives living with us or nearby, and mostly if our parents have any affiliation with a political party and express political views. I am almost thirteen, a serious girl who comes from the war experience, and quite suspicious of strangers asking such questions.

Instead of writing the truth about my family, I decide to make up some interesting stories about politicians and artists who frequently visit our house to impress Eva néni and my classmates when my turn to read comes. One day, Eva néni informs us that soon we will have to hand in our diaries for her to read. I feel uneasy.

"Zsuzsa," I ask, "do you think Eva néni is spying on us?" Zsuzsa is not sure but she too knows that something serious is going on. I need not wonder long. Mother always finds out everything. One day when I come home, she is standing in the hallway waving my diary and screaming. Obviously, she read it, including all the untrue stories meant to impress Eva néni. "You are going to land Pista and me in jail if anybody reads the lies you have written," she yells. "Did you think of that!"

"It's an assignment and we have to hand it in," I say.

"How dare they!" she screams. "How dare they ask you to inform on us."

She instructs me to write a new diary, without describing any important details of our lives.

I am really upset. Pista tries to explain his understanding of the situation to me. "Hungary's occupation by the Russians means a Communist takeover of our government and the indoctrination of our people according to the Soviet model."

"It's not what our gym program is all about," I tell him. "We do many good and interesting things in our cell to work for a better new world."

Pista looks at me and shakes his head. "See how subtly indoctrinated your mind already is with left-wing ideology? And the diary is how they gather information for the files of the secret police of the future totalitarian regime."

I do not want to believe it. He is scaring me. I really like most of the things that we do in my gym program. We go to our May Day parade with streamers and thousands of us perform in one of the fields outside Budapest. We have a marching band. We sing songs together. We go on field trips and tell stories around campfires. I feel wonderful to be part of it.

"What do you talk about with the older girls who head your group?" Pista asks.

I'm a little embarrassed but tell him anyway. "We talk about equality and justice for all. We talk about the life of the working man and how to make it better."

"Those are beautiful ideas, and it would be a wonderful world if they could be made to work," he says, "but they don't. They have already failed. You are almost thirteen and mature enough to examine carefully what is realistic and what is not."

He looks at me and stops talking. I think he realizes that I am not sure what he means, or maybe I just don't want to hear it. But now, when I am at school, I start to recognize the attempts of the program to indoctrinate. In spite of that, I stay intrigued and interested in the principles of a socialist system. I participate in most programs, sometimes reluctantly and sometimes with a fair amount of enthusiasm. I want to be part of building a better world.

My budding interest in a new political system is not shared by the adults I know. One night, I overhear Mother talking to Pista. "Let's not make a mistake again and wait too long. We should have left Hungary before the war or before the Nazis took over, but we missed that opportunity. This time we have to make sure to leave before the Communists close the borders to the west, or we will never ever be able to live a normal life."

"I agree," Pista says. "Since I am an Austrian citizen, we are able to leave, but we have to find out what I and my family are allowed to take out of the country. And we need to do it before the next election."

"I am also concerned about my mother," Mother continues. "I am not sure if she will ever be healthy enough to travel."

I am frightened when I hear this. I was not aware that my grandmother is so sick, and I was not aware that we want to leave Hungary. We have recently moved into this beautiful house. I am doing well in school. I have some friends. I have my father, and I certainly can't see what is wrong with a socialist takeover. I think that equality and justice are noble principles, and that is what the new politicians propose to give us once elected. Why is that so dangerous? I don't understand.

The next day, Zsuzsa and I have a conversation about the situation. "My father too wants to get out of this country as fast as possible," she says, "before we can no longer leave. But he says his assets are all tied up here, and he is trying to get some of them out of the country before the borders close."

So it is true that we are in some kind of danger again.

A few weeks later, Grandmother Adél calls me into her room. She tells me about one piece of the shrapnel in her leg, which is working its way to the surface and is giving her a fair amount of pain. Grandmother has been bedridden now for the past several weeks and she also stayed at the hospital for a few days just recently. She has been diagnosed with terminal leukemia.

"Sit on my bed," she says. "I expect to die soon. I hope I am going to die soon enough so that you and the family can escape." Her talking of her death makes me want to cry.

"Please don't talk like that," I tell her. "I'm sure you will get well again. I don't want you to die. You are the only person who really cares about me. You always take my side when Mother attacks me. I can't imagine life without you. You have to come with us when we leave."

She is stroking my hair, which is her habit. She looks at me very sadly and says, "I am so sorry, but I don't think that I will make it. I am most upset about having to leave you to your mother. She is my daughter, but she is not a good person. She is cruel and demanding and cannot be kind. Please remember that I would stay with you if I could, and know in your heart that I love you." I start to cry. She keeps on stroking my hair and tells me nice things until I fall asleep lying next to her on the bed.

I ask Mother whether we are really leaving. "Yes, we are," she says, "but you mustn't tell anyone. Pista is an Austrian citizen, and so we have certain privileges. The government accepts the fact that we are not leaving Hungary but we are going home to Austria. The advantage is that we can take our possessions with us, unless they are valuable antiques, art, or jewelry."

I am more and more upset. Are we going, or are we not? Again and again at dinner it is repeated that we cannot leave Grandmother Adél behind. I realize that we are just waiting for her to die.

Grandmother Adél's next hospital stay is not very long. Mother comes home one day crying and tells me that she died peacefully that morning. I am devastated. She is dead and we are going to leave Budapest and my father. I feel like an orphan.

"She will be buried," Mother informs me, "next to your grandfather Béla bácsi in the Jewish cemetery tomorrow morning."

"What time?" I ask. "I will miss school. I will need a note for that."

"You're not going to the funeral," she says. "And please don't even talk about it to anyone."

"Why am I not allowed to go to the funeral?" I ask. Mother says I am too young, but how can I be too young? I saw many people die in the war. At first I can't figure this out, but then I do. Nobody in my school or among my friends other than Zsuzsa is to know that my Grandmother Adél is buried in the Jewish cemetery. I start to argue with Mother. "I would like to accompany her to her resting place." But the answer remains no.

"And remember not to tell your friends," says Mother. "We don't ever want anybody to know that our family was Jewish."

I spend the morning at school trying to hide my sorrow. Only Zsuzsa knows and she tries to console me on the way home. Mother is crying when she comes home from the funeral and spends the rest of the day in her room.

The preparation for leaving Hungary gears up. Everything has to be done secretly because Mother is afraid that my father will not give her permission to take me out of the country. We have already sold the artwork and antiques that we can't take with us. Pista's inheritance of a bag of diamonds represents our future security. The diamonds will have to be smuggled across the border.

There are two things we worry about—one is the diamonds and the other is my status as a Hungarian citizen. Since I was never adopted by Pista, I do not qualify for Austrian citizenship like my mother and my half-sister, Katika. There are many discussions on how to make sure that I get to Austria too. At the Austrian passport office, my mother, always bold, takes a chance and submits my name along with Katika's as her and Pista's children. Fortunately, the officials do not bother to check our ages because they would discover that I was far too old to be Mother and Pista's child, as Pista was still living in Austria when I was born. Both my name and Katika's are entered into Mother's passport. She comes home triumphantly waving the document.

The day of departure arrives. We are traveling by train, and the contents of the house will follow and arrive in Vienna within a few weeks. The four of us and two large suitcases head for the station. That morning, some of the largest diamonds were tied into tiny rubber packages that Mother swallowed, under the supervision of her doctor, a family friend. This is the way our fortune is to accompany us to our new destination. I keep looking at Mother to see how she is feeling. She looks beautiful and elegant. She is wearing a new traveling suit, custom-made especially for the occasion—a green and beige checked tweed skirt with a beige silk blouse and a matching coat that is reversible. The pain she must be feeling in her stomach does not show on her face.

The trip to Vienna is only three and a half hours. Crossing the border, in spite of all of our fears, turns out to be easy and fast. Passport control finds all of our papers in order. When the train moves on, we are in Austria. Pista and Mother are hugging in our compartment and Mother cries for joy. Only I am sad. Secretly leaving all that I love—my father, my friends, my school and the exciting activities I enjoyed—makes me feel like an orphan, not knowing what my new life is going to be.

We arrive in Vienna and stay in a rooming house in the American zone of the city. The next few days are spent watching Mother sit on a potty, waiting for the diamonds to drop.

Vienna in 1948 is divided into four occupied zones: Russian, French, British, and American. It is difficult to get around because it is dangerous for us to cross into a Russian zone, which sometimes is just across the street, for fear of being deported back to Hungary. This I don't understand. If Pista is Austrian, how can they deport us? But nevertheless, we live cautiously and in fear.

A few days later, after all the diamonds have been retrieved and Mother is back on a regular diet, our Vienna life starts at full speed. We rent a beautiful big apartment in the center of the city and as soon as our furniture arrives, we move in.

Mother has a job waiting for her with Aunt Philippine and

Uncle Sandor Lehr, an older Viennese couple. Aunt Philippine is related to my mother. I could never figure out how, but I was told it goes back a long time. Mother even stayed with them as a young girl when she visited Vienna before the war. When we first go to their apartment in the Lindengasse, a good neighborhood of Vienna, I love it because they own a blue and yellow canary called Pepsi whose limited vocabulary consists of a sentence identifying herself: "Ich bin die Pepsi Lehr aus der Lindengasse." In between beautiful songs, she repeats this sentence often. I really love that bird.

The Lehrs, who are Jewish, own a small clothing manufacturing plant. It is now back in their possession after having been taken over by the Nazi government during the war. It is in the process of going under. Mother has been engaged to try to turn it around.

Katika, who is now six years old, is registered at a nearby school. It is decided that as I am almost fourteen, it would be better for me to be in a boarding school, so I can concentrate on my education and to speed up my fluency in the German language. Accordingly, I am enrolled in a convent school nearby, run by the Ursuline Sisters. I hate it from the first day. I hate the discipline; I hate the Mass every morning, the strict study hours in the afternoon, and the lack of outdoor activities. I miss my father and my life and friends in Budapest.

This is the beginning of my new indoctrination—this time as a pacticing Catholic.

CHAPTER THIRTEEN

THE CONVENTS IN VIENNA AND ST. PÖLTEN

• 1948–1949 •

LEARNING GERMAN DOES NOT seem to be too difficult for me. I am in my regular class according to my age. The little chapel where we go to daily Mass is beautiful, and being fond of old things, I enjoy the architecture and the paintings. I even enjoy the beauty of the iron bars on the small rectangular windows in the bedrooms where we sleep. I wonder why we need bars on small windows on the third floor of the building. The bars are of very old hand-forged wrought iron, and they curve in a certain way that is quite beautiful. They remind me of castles instead of prisons.

What feels like prison is the daily routine of having to get up every morning at six thirty to be at Mass at seven o'clock. After Mass and breakfast, classes start at eight thirty, which is when we are joined by the day students who are lucky enough to go home in the afternoon when school is over. We have another prayer session after lunch, which marks the beginning of the study period. We stop at five thirty for a novena and a walk in the courtyard. We cannot go outside the convent grounds. After dinner, we go to the recreation room where we can read from the convent library, sketch and paint with the limited supplies, or knit and embroider, all under the supervision of eagle-eyed nuns. All of our teachers are nuns. It is a strict order. They are well educated but it hurts them to smile. I don't have any warm feelings about them.

I befriend a couple of the girls, but with my limited language skills it is difficult to carry on a friendship. Still, one girl in particular, Yvonne, makes an effort and talks to me often. She is a day student and seems older than the rest of us. She confides in me that she wears lipstick when she is not in school, which of course is strictly forbidden even outside the premises. One day she asks me, "Would you do me a favor, please?"

"Of course," I say.

"Would you receive a letter that someone will hand you in the chapel tomorrow during morning prayers? You have to stand by the holy water. Someone will hand it to you. It is for me, but I will not be there since I do not come to school until after prayers."

"Of course, I'll do it," I say. I feel good about being asked as if her confiding in me is a special sign of acceptance.

The next morning, I stand near the holy water as instructed and somebody from behind slides a letter into my hand. By the time I turn, I can't tell who gave me the letter. It is a small envelope so I slide it in my pocket. I rejoin my class at the front of the chapel and participate in the rest of the Mass.

Barely out of chapel on my way to breakfast, one of the head nuns approaches me. "What did somebody give you in the chapel?" she says.

"Just a letter," I say.

"Who is it from?" she wants to know.

Now I am getting anxious. "I don't know who it is from," I answer truthfully. "It is not for me."

By now the nun has taken the letter, opened it, and is in the process of reading it. I have a sense that something is terribly wrong, but I have no idea what it could be. When the nun finishes reading the letter, she grabs me by the arm. "We go to Mother Superior right now." She drags me off to Mother Superior's office.

Mother Superior reads the letter, looks at me, and asks, "Who is this man you are seeing?"

"What man?" I say.

"The one who wrote the letter."

"I don't know who wrote the letter."

"So how come you have the letter?" she asks.

I'm getting frightened. I really don't know what to say, but I repeat the same thing again and again. "I do not know who wrote the letter. I am doing a favor for a friend who asked me to receive it."

"Who is the friend who asked you to receive the letter?"

I realize that something in that letter must be very bad. "I can assure you the letter was not for me. I cannot tell you who it is for because I cannot betray a friend."

"Do you realize," says Mother Superior, "that I have to call your mother? Maybe she can convince you to tell us who the letter was for."

I am made to wait in the office until Mother gets there. When she does, she reads the letter and I can tell that she is upset.

"Who the hell wrote you this letter?" she says in a high-pitched voice.

"The letter is not for me, Mother. I don't know who wrote it."

"Okay, my dear," she says. "Then who is the letter for?"

"I cannot and will not tell you. I cannot betray a friend."

Discussions follow between Mother Superior and my mother

about how to find out whom the letter was from and to whom it was addressed if it is true that it was not for me. Mother Superior turns to me and explains the consequences of my not telling them everything. If I don't tell them whom the letter was for, they will assume it was for me. And if it was for me, judging by the contents, they do not want me in this school.

My mother makes a last-ditch effort and hisses at me, "Don't be stupid. Tell them whom it was for. Do you realize you are being thrown out of school? Don't sacrifice your future for a selfish friend."

"No, Mother," I say. "I cannot betray her and I cannot believe that you and Mother Superior would want me to be so dishonorable as to betray someone's trust. I am telling the truth. The letter wasn't for me. I do not know whom it was from, and I will not tell you whom it was for."

Mother Superior says again and again that she will have to expel me, and my mother continuously reminds me of stupidity. She literally drags me out of the building and back to our apartment. All the way she tries to convince me to give up the name. "You only have to mention the name. I'll go and see Mother Superior and tell her. Just give me the name."

By the time we get home, Mother is so angry that she is shaking me, and I am afraid that the next thing she will do is beat me. I free myself from her grip and head to my room. I am truly upset because these adults want me to do dishonorable things, like give up a friend. But I am also angry at Yvonne because, after all, why did she not receive the letter herself? She is a day student; she could have received the letter outside of school. And I am angry at Mother Superior because I think she should have gone to the class and asked openly who was supposed to receive the letter. But by the time I realize that I will sleep in my own bed tonight and I don't have to go back to the Ursuline

Sisters and their rigid discipline, I am not that unhappy. I wonder what my next school is going to be like. I'm hoping for a day school somewhere near our apartment.

Mother seems to believe me, without saying so. I can tell she too is upset with the nuns for assuming my guilt.

"I am curious what is in that letter," I say.

"It is not a love letter," she says. "It is dirty." She makes that face that signifies *disgusting*. She uses that expression often when referring to boys who want to "get you."

Mother tells me a few days later that she tried to enroll me in two schools. They both asked for references and wanted to know why I was changing schools so early in the year. Obviously, the references were not very good because they refused to enroll me. "The wrath of the nuns," I say, but Mother does not even smile. Pista starts to laugh but he is not allowed. Mother gives him a dirty look and he stops.

She continues to conduct research about the availability of other schools while I enjoy my freedom. I go to the Stadtpark and meet some girls and boys, play ball, and have some fun, but not for too long since for my punishment, I am allowed to stay away from home for only two hours during the day and not at all after eight o'clock in the evening. But I'm glad I have some time for reading. After a few days, Mother starts packing some of my things and informs me that we are going on a trip. Judging by her voice and her attitude, I'm suspicious. I'm sure that nothing good is waiting for me at the end of this trip.

Pista is driving us in the new Peugeot that they just bought. Mother explains about my new school. She says, "This school is even more expensive than the other. There are only twenty girls your age boarding in the school. It is known as a school for problem girls."

What did she say? I am flabbergasted. Sitting in the back of the car, I can't believe what I just heard. I ask her, "How come you enrolled me in a school like that?"

"With the references you got, no other school would take you. You are lucky," she says, "that I am willing to spend this kind of money on your education. I believe that the letter was truly not for you. But I am upset by your stupidity."

It feels good to hear that she believes my side of the story, but I am not so sure about my "stupidity." A sermon on boys follows. She tells me that I am too young to deal with boys. Part of the reason she wants me in a strict convent environment is to keep me safe and protect me from boys. Nothing should distract me from my studies. I keep quiet. I don't know where all of this comes from. How can she forget that I was in the war with her? I saw more than I care to remember. How can she speak to me as if to a child? How can she think that locking me up in a convent will be good for me? I am desperately upset.

She is still droning on. I bring my attention back to what she is saying and catch a few more sentences, particularly the last one that I have heard many times before and that is very important to her: "You have to be well-behaved so that we can get back to normal life."

What does she mean by "normal life"? Is it normal to tell lies about everything—our origins, our history, our family—even now when the war is over? In Mother's opinion, as I have heard before, pretending to be what we are not is precisely the way to achieve a normal life.

As we approach the convent, Mother is still carrying on about "normal." Listening to her has made this the longest one-hour drive I have ever been on. We arrive in the venerable old city of St. Pölten, west of Vienna, and stop in the courtyard of a beautiful, undamaged building that is a few hundred years old. When the large ancient wooden doors of the main building open, I feel intimidated looking down a long corridor with shiny floors you might easily slip on. On the walls hang many religious paintings. I step carefully and try not to make any noise. I feel like whispering and hope Mother won't talk too loudly.

My anxiety is broken by the appearance a large friendly nun who takes charge of me almost immediately. She allows me only one minute to say goodbye to Mother and Pista, which is fine because our goodbyes are normally not lengthy or emotional. We don't hug. We don't kiss. Since they are mad at me for being expelled, this time I don't even get a little peck on the cheek.

The friendly, smiling nun introduces herself as Sister Cecilia. She is part of a teaching order called Englishe Fräulein. The day school is for students in grades one to six. The "problem girls" are all my age, around fourteen, and we are the only boarding students. Our classrooms are separate from the rest of the school. While she escorts me to my dormitory, Sister Cecilia talks to me in rapid German, which somehow I understand. There are twenty cubicles separated by curtains, each with a bed, a nightstand with a small sink, and a little cabinet underneath. Sister takes my bag and helps me unpack the things I was allowed to bring: a few pairs of underwear, one or two bras, and a nightgown. I didn't bring any other clothes apart from what I am wearing, a shirt and sweater and jacket. Those were the instructions, according to my mother, as the school will assign a uniform to me.

Our next stop is the room with the uniforms. Another friendly nun there looks at me and assesses the size I need. Here and there, I understand what they are saying and take pleasure to know that my fluency in German is improving. It is strange, but this convent is supposed to be stricter than the one in Vienna, dealing with girls who might not want to stay here. Yet I feel much less restricted and am quite at home with the two friendly nuns who are looking after my orientation.

The uniform consists of a partially pleated navy skirt, a white blouse, and a navy cardigan that I try on. It feels too big but there are no mirrors anywhere so I can't be sure. My shoes are the only thing I am allowed to keep.

Sister Cecilia, apparently, is also in charge of taking me on a tour of the various classrooms. It is midafternoon and there are no classes in session. We go to see the dining room, which is quite small since there are only twenty boarding students. Next, we stop to see the bathroom and several cubicles of toilets. Sister tells me that we are allowed a bath once a week, usually on Friday.

I think I misunderstand and ask in German, "Nur am Freitag?"

"Jawohl," says Sister, and there is no doubt: bath is only once a week on Friday.

We turn around and go back to the library, which houses the study room. Before we go in, Sister Cecilia alerts me that all my fellow students are in the study room because in the afternoons all the girls are expected to study for four hours.

When she opens the door to the study, the first thing I notice is the stale and musty air. I immediately connect it to the rule of one bath a week. But soon it does not seem important because several of the girls are approaching to greet me. I can't believe how friendly everyone is here. Sister tells the girls my name and asks them to show me around. She smiles at me once more and leaves. I notice another nun sitting at the far end of the room, overlooking the procedures. One of the girls takes me to her and introduces me as "the new student." Sister Renata welcomes me, and although she doesn't have a smiling face, she gives the impression of being friendly. She gets up from her elevated perch and steps down, showing me where my seat will be at one of the long tables. I'm sitting with a set of twins who look so alike that it is totally impossible to tell them apart, especially at first glance. Everything on them is identical, even the creases on the sleeves of their shirts and the strand of hair hanging down in front of their eyes. The fourth girl at my table is very large and looks like an overgrown baby. I'm sure when she wears her own clothes, she wears pink and blue.

Sister Renata tells me to sit down and she will bring me some of my work material, which I have to deliver back to her before I leave the study room when we go for dinner. The study room has fairly strict rules, she tells me—some talking in a low voice is allowed but not for long. She will permit one or two trips to the bathroom in the span of the four-hour study session, but only one girl at a time can leave the room. There is not much walking around permitted. "If you run short of working material," Sister Renata says, "you may come to my desk and I will replenish your supplies."

I am trying to familiarize myself with the papers she gives me. There are some with mathematical problems and some that ask you to write a short essay. I'm not doing that badly on the mathematics, but I'm certainly not doing well on writing an essay in German. And I'm hungry. I can hardly wait to go to the dining room for dinner. But first we have to go and pray. Sister Renata rings the bell and we all get up and go to the chapel for a short prayer.

Finally, we are on our way to the dining room. More introductions follow. I try to keep near the twins to know where to sit and what to do. We are being served at our table. The girls inform me that the nuns who are serving us are not really nuns yet; they are novices. They have different light-colored habits and no veil. The novices do most of the work. Two bring the food out on big trays, and another two serve each of the girls. I look at my plate and I'm worried. It doesn't look like enough food to me.

I ask one of the girls sitting near me, "Do we eat anything else or do we get second helpings?"

"You can get more bread if you are hungry. We also have dessert."

Being used to generous helpings, the food does not seem to be adequate. I ask one of the twins, "Can you bring some food and keep it somewhere?"

"Not really," she says. "If they find it, they will confiscate it."

"I guess you have to eat a lot when you go home."

But that is the wrong first impression. Our three meals turn out to be ample, especially breakfast—lots of bread, butter that I suspect is margarine, eggs (soft-boiled or as an omelet), with slabs of bacon or smoked ham from the bone. This meal is the only one served buffet style and the quantities are unlimited. The tea comes in large urns already mixed with milk and sugar.

The other two meals are progressively less substantial. Lunch is soup, meat, potatoes, vegetables, and a small dessert. There are no choices and the quantities are predetermined as it all comes to the table in a bowl or on a plate. Dinner is the smallest meal: grains and baked goods served with a compote of fruits or vegetables cooked (and cooked and cooked) served usually with a cheese sauce. You can ask for more bread if you are still hungry.

Living in this convent is pleasant compared to the one in the city. I think Mother misunderstood the words "problem girls" as being backward or of low intelligence or of some unacceptable behavior for good Christian girls, which turns out not to be the case at all. About half of the girls are nonpaying cases, mostly

from local families, farmers, or small businessmen, affiliated with
the church but unable to pay even a modest fee for their children's Catholic education.

Other boarders do come from "problem" homes, well-kept
secrets that do not stay secrets for long—a drunk and dangerous
father, an absent mother (who ran away never to be heard of
again, leaving a few children behind). And there's Mary "the
orphan," who is very nice but has no home to go to on the weekends we go home because her parents are working in another
country.

The curriculum of the school has an excellent reputation. I
think that is the reason for the other half of the boarding school
population: girls from Vienna, daughters of lawyers, doctors, and
businessmen, ardent Catholics all and supporters of the order.
They prefer to keep their daughters out of the city, away from the
difficulties of the capital's many postwar problems. The four zones
of occupation in Vienna make it difficult to get around. Guards
on many corners are entitled to ask for ID, even of children from
the ages of ten years up. Due to these problems, country schools
and country convent schools are in particularly great demand.

After I become familiar with what is going on, I wonder how
my mother got me accepted to this prestigious institution, especially with my "record." When I ask, Mother does not give an
explanation, except that she reminds me that she always finds a
way. I think that she must have made a sizable donation to the
order, as the good Catholic woman she is pretending to be, before even applying for my admission. I don't think that my alleged record was even presented. Nobody ever brings it up.

It is true that the convent is stricter than the one in the city.
There are more rules and regulations, and they are enforced.
Running on the long corridors is forbidden and the penalty is

the saying of five rosaries in the chapel. Reciting rosaries is the penalty for almost everything, for taking too long to get ready for bed or for talking or whispering in the dormitory after lights out. A Sister is living in a small room at the entrance to the dorm with her windows mostly open to listen and make sure that dorm rules are kept. She even counts the number of trips the girls take to the bathroom during the night.

In spite of all that, I'm quite comfortable here. I appreciate the all-pervasive friendliness that exists even when punishments are doled out. The one serious problem I have has to do with cleanliness. One bath a week is inadequate for anyone. I do not understand why we clean everything around us until all is shiny clean, except our bodies, ourselves.

When the first bath night arrives, I can hardly wait. I ask Alice, one of the girls, whether she is excited. She just makes a face and says, "You'll see."

The Sister in charge of our baths divides us into groups of five. We march into the bathroom, where we are instructed to drop our uniforms and put them in a basket for the laundry. But then we are to pick up a long cotton shirt to put on before removing our underwear. When questioned, the Sister says, "You're really not supposed to see your naked body." I can't believe this is happening. I turn around, ready to make an argument, but I think better. I do not wish to be punished with reciting one hundred rosaries. In the meantime, we fill our appointed tubs with hot water and close the curtains around our cubicles before we get into the tub. It feels so good to sit in a bath, but it is hard to get clean with the shirt floating around in the tub. There is another thing that we have to do during our bath and that is reciting the rosary in a loud steady voice. I am wondering why we are doing that.

Suddenly, there is a commotion in the next cubicle. I hear Sister pulling the curtain open and asking Alice, who is in that cubicle, why her voice is faltering. I hear Sister's sermon to Alice about the sinfulness of touching her body. Alice is sent to Mother Superior for her reprimand.

By the time the rosary is over, the water is getting cold. We get out of the tub and wrap a towel around us before we remove the wet shirt. We put on clean underwear and our uniforms that are waiting for us on the chairs. We clean the bathtubs, faucets and all, until they are really shiny. The floor is quickly mopped by some of the novices who were waiting outside. The bathroom is ready for the next group of girls.

"Going home weekend" comes around faster than I expected. I am allowed to leave on Friday since I live in the city. I forgo the bath because Pista arrives at five o'clock and wants to leave as soon as possible. Even though his mother was a nun, he seems quite uncomfortable around them no matter how friendly they are.

Mother is not with him. She is too busy at the "salon," a custom dressmaking business that she started at home. She is designing and selling a small collection of women's clothing that she calls "Postwar Fashion and Prewar Quality," which is selling quite well. She is an innovator and at the forefront of ready-made clothing in postwar Vienna. All of the clothes are designed and cut by my mother. She goes to Paris for inspiration. Her custom salon at home is a sideline to the clothing factory where she works for Aunt Philippine and Uncle Sandor. Pista too has found a good job with an export-import company.

Katika is in the car waiting for me. I have not seen her in more than a month and miss her. She seems to have missed me too. I am the only person with whom she can be without a lot of drama. She has developed into a high-energy, mischievous six-year-old given to pranks and intentional bad behavior, mostly directed at Mother, who reacts with anger and yells and screams. Often, Pista intervenes. "Leave her alone," he hisses, trembling uncontrollably. "She's just a child." Pista is very protective of Katika and comes to her rescue every time. He sometimes tries to do the same for me when Mother goes off the deep end, but the results are different. Mother turns on him, telling him to keep out of her business. After all, I am not his daughter and taking my side, even if it is justified, represents major disloyalty to her. I know that there is no reasonable conversation when she is on her warpath. I try to keep quiet.

But now I am in the car with Katika, getting details from her about her school, her friends, her activities. Mother has engaged a "governess" for weekday afternoons who takes Katika for walks in the park, helps her with her first-grade homework, and keeps her busy and out of Mother's hair.

Pista is very much a part of the conversation in the car. He makes his stupid, funny jokes as usual and we laugh a lot. It makes me happy that the funny part of his personality has reemerged. We arrive in the city after several detours to avoid the Russian zones. When we get to the apartment, Mother immediately sends me to the bathroom for a long warm bath. I put on clean underwear and clothing and it feels wonderful. We sit down at the table for dinner. I start to make the sign of the cross. It's a habit I picked up at meals at the convent. I don't even realize what I am doing until I notice Pista and Mother staring at me, horrified. She doesn't have to say anything. Her angry look makes me stop mid-cross.

During dinner, I'm queried about my school, my classes, and my "hard-to-educate" friends. It is a difficult conversation because Katika is disruptive. She wants more attention so she fingers her food, jumps up from the table (which is strictly forbidden), wants something else to eat, and finally starts crying. Mother turns to me and says, "Why don't you stop her? She usually listens to you."

Going back to St. Pölten on Sunday seems like a pleasant occurrence. I'm surprised how good I feel returning. The rest of the year goes by fast. My language skills have greatly improved, and my final grades put me close to the top of the class.

CHAPTER FOURTEEN

VIENNA

• Summer 1949 •

I'M NOT LOOKING FORWARD to going home for the summer and being exposed to my mother's never-ending wrath. I'm not sure that I am looking forward to her summer plans for me either. She volunteered me as a helper at the summer camp for six- to twelve-year-olds where my sister is going. Mother has convinced the director that Katika is a difficult child and that I am the person who can best handle her. A deal has been struck. They will charge half of what they normally charge and I am to help out with Katika and also with some of the other kids. I find the idea offensive. I really do not want to go and be a babysitter for a bunch of little kids. I have tried to convince Mother to let me stay in Vienna and find something to do over the summer months. But she is determined. I cannot stay home.

The camp is in a small village called Velden on the shores of the Wörthersee, one of the loveliest lakes in Austria. I try to console myself with the prospect of the activities around the lake, swimming and sailing. But there are not many organized activities offered by the camp, as all the children are young. There are swimming lessons, ball games, and excursions to the surrounding area. I have a lot of free time to go to the lake by myself, and I eventually get to know and hang out with the sailing crowd. I meet a few people with boats, particularly the brothers Peter and Wolfgang, who are nineteen and twenty-one, respectively and own one of the most beautiful boats on the lake. Peter is extremely handsome, tall with blue eyes, light-brown hair, and a gorgeous suntan. Wolfgang is quiet but pays attention to everybody and can on occasion be very funny. Of course, I am developing a major crush on Peter. We all have a very good time but when older girls are around, Peter barely notices me. I look eighteen, as everybody tells me, but I am only fifteen and everybody knows that too.

One morning when I come down to the lake, their boat is not there. Wolfgang is sitting on the dock. "Hello, hello, hello. You look especially lovely today" is his greeting. Usually, he is not so expansive.

"Where is the boat?" I ask.

"What boat?"

"Stop trying to be funny," I reply. "Where is the boat and where is Peter?"

"Peter went sailing with the boat," he states, as if that was really obvious and I am asking a stupid question.

My heart sinks. A pretty eighteen-year-old girl named Sissy has been hanging around with us the last few days. I did not think much of her. She liked being silly and laughing a lot, mostly for no reason that I could see. Until now, I did not think that Peter took her seriously. Wolfgang is eyeing me, knowing that I will ask the inevitable question that should not be asked: "Did he take Sissy with him?"

"Yes," Wolfgang solemnly answers, "and Peter said not to expect them back for quite a while."

I am dumbstruck, devastated. In the past few weeks, Peter, Wolfgang, and I spent a lot of time together and had a very good time. I thought Peter liked me. I was starting to consider myself his girlfriend. Wolfgang is walking away from the dock. "Come, let's go," he says to me. He does not look too happy either and I realize that he too is being excluded from his brother's life.

I walk with him. "Where are we going?" I want to know.

"Back to my house," he says, "where you can cry in peace. Don't worry," he continues. "You know you can trust me." I am surprised that he knows how close I am to crying and that he understands.

I cry and cry about Peter and how he can do this to me. After all, I am prettier than Sissy and smarter too. Wolfgang is a good listener, and he gives me a handkerchief for my tears. Soon, I am telling him about my other troubles, mostly about Mother and my battles with her. The more I talk, the more I cry, angry and disappointed with everything in my life.

Wolfgang interrupts and says, "I'll bring you something to drink. You'll feel better." He hands me a small glass and when I smell it, I know it is schnapps. "You have to swallow it all at once," he instructs. It goes down fast, although it burns my throat and then my stomach. But soon I start to calm down and feel a little better. I stop talking about all the problems in my life and ask Wolfgang for more of his "remedy." He is reluctant but gives it to me anyway and says, "You better go. You don't want to get into trouble being late for lunch."

I am not late but still get into trouble when I get back. I am quite tipsy and it is clear to everyone that I have had a few drinks. And so the interrogation begins. Where? How? Who? At first, I comply, but soon a sense of danger overcomes me and I refuse to answer any more questions. I am sent to my room and

I go to sleep. When I wake up, it is late afternoon and my mother is standing in my room.

"What, oh what did you do?" Apparently, I caused quite a scandal, she was told when they called her to come immediately. Pista drove her down but he is waiting in the car. My mother wants to know all of the details of what has actually happened. She wants to know whom I got drunk with, where it happened, and then of course the most important question: "Did he touch you?"

"What did you say?" I do not understand why she is asking me that question. "Nothing happened. I had two schnapps with a friend and got a little drunk."

"Did you sleep with the guy?" Mother asks abruptly.

"What are you talking about? It was still early in the morning, around eleven."

"Don't be impertinent," my mother says and turns to the director, who has just entered the room. "What do you want to know?"

"Nothing," she says. "I want you to take her home. We don't want her here anymore. But you need to sign these papers that we are not responsible if Erika contracted an illness or became pregnant due to her behavior on this date."

So I am home before the end of the summer. Mother has asked me several times since I have been home if I have been touched. "Where was it again he tried to touch you? Was it between your legs?" She tries to trap me, acting as if I have already admitted it but she is not sure she remembers it correctly. I don't fall for the bait, but it makes me feel bad. Next time she tries it, I tell her to get off my back. She reminds me it is the second time I have been expelled since we have arrived in Vienna and starts to yell hateful and vulgar words—*whore, drunk, liar*. She does not care how much she hurts me. She just goes on and on. I'm going to have a miserable rest of the summer but something unexpected happens that changes everything.

Very early one morning a few days after the "incident" at camp, there is a *bang, bang* and then an even louder *bang*, and I am fully awake. I'm frightened, panicked. I'm convinced it's the Gestapo or the Arrow Cross coming to get me. They will say that they are going to move me to the ghetto, but I know the truth. They will take me to the camps or the Danube River.

But the banging does not sound too violent, and I hear voices arguing. It can't be the Gestapo or the Arrow Cross—nobody in their right mind would talk back to the Gestapo or the Arrow Cross. What is actually going on? I am now fully awake and realize that this is not Budapest, Hungary, in 1944, where those deadly raids took place. It's Vienna, Austria, in 1949, where we assume we are safe. Then I hear a man's voice demanding in Hungarian to be let in the door because he has relatives in the building. I know that voice. It sounds like my father. My father?!

I jump out of bed and run to the balcony, which spans the length of the apartment and overlooks the large front entrance. Mother is there on the balcony already, leaning over the stone balustrades. She is yelling at the concierge, "Let those people in." I look down, and although it is four o'clock in the morning and still dark, the street lights illuminate our entrance well. It is my father and he is not alone. Standing next to him is Kato néni, my grandmother.

The commotion downstairs subsides. Our concierge, a feisty old Viennese woman, is always ready to fight verbally and I think physically too. She talks to my father through the peephole in the gate. As is customary in Vienna, the tenants have no keys to the building's main entrance. After eleven o'clock at night, everyone has to ring the bell in order to enter. This annoying procedure ensures security for the tenants, as well as additional income for the concierge in the form of tips. She is frightening to me but she melts when she sees Pista, who runs downstairs to the front entrance and reassures her in his native Viennese that these are indeed legitimate visitors. He apologizes to her for the inconvenience we are causing, and she finally agrees to open the gate. Mother and I observe the proceedings from the balcony.

People have opened a few windows across the street to see what is going on, especially since my irrepressible grandmother, tired of waiting, starts to sing as she always does to help resolve situations. Mother says to me in a loud whisper, "We'll have to teach her to shut up!" I disagree. I love my singing grandmother but understand that her performances could be dangerous in this divided city, where crossing the street at the wrong corner can have serious consequences for refugees without proper papers who have stepped into Russian territory.

Finally, Father and Kato néni are at the front door of our apartment. They come in and we see them in the light of the entrance hall, and I notice the signs of the ordeal they must have been through escaping to Vienna. When Kato néni hugs me, I can feel the dirt sticking to her clothes. She is crying now. "Tears of happiness," she says. But she is holding on to me because her knees are buckling and I'm afraid that she will collapse.

My father's reactions are different. "Good to see you, good to see you," he says to all of us and repeats it again and again. I think he cannot yet believe that they really are in Vienna. Whatever perils their escape entailed, they survived, and they have now arrived in a relatively safe place. I look at this dirty, tired person, who can barely stand up but is too agitated to sit down, fighting back his tears as he looks around. He sees his former wife (my mother), Pista (my stepfather), and me, his fifteen-year-old daughter, and says, "They had a gun to her head." He is looking at my grandmother, who is quite exhausted sitting in our big armchair falling asleep, clutching her battered old purse.

Haltingly, he continues through his tears to tell us the story of their escape from Communist Hungary to Austria through closed borders. For large sums of money, you could be smuggled across the electrified wire fences. Father decided to leave Hungary by this means. The question was how to find "reliable smugglers" so you could be sure you would eventually arrive at your destination. "The guides I contracted were recommended with a pretty good track record," my father says. "Anni néni decided not to leave the country. We got divorced and I gave her the apartment in Budapest." Getting ready to leave took a while. Father talks about how difficult it was to sell his assets, to get enough money to pay the smugglers, and to keep everything a secret so as not to jeopardize their departure.

"I had to make sure that the smugglers knew that Kato cannot walk far. They had to bring us to a break in the electrified wire fence on the border where we could get through without too much walking. When we left Budapest with a car and driver provided by the smugglers, everything was fine until we were walking with our two guides toward the opening in the electrified fence. A loud voice stopped us just as we were handing the last part of our payment to the smugglers."

Then, Father said somebody yelled, "Freeze, freeze." He went on with his story. "The smugglers stopped for a minute, then tried to run when a second man in the uniform of a border guard materialized. He had a gun and commanded the smugglers to hand over the money they had just received from us. They complied and then ran away. The man with the gun and the one behind him, who was brandishing a rifle, came closer to us and demanded money from us too. When I said I didn't have any, one of them put his gun to Kato's head and said, 'Either you give us what you have or she's dead.'"

Father said he removed a package from under his shirt and handed it to them. It was foreign currency and valuable stocks worth a lot of money. He and Kato néni also had cash that she carried in her big black purse that she was clutching. Father was sure once they gave up the valuables, two shots would ring out, one for him and one for her. But that's not what happened. When Father handed over what he had and Kato néni emptied her purse of all the cash she was carrying, the two border guards left without any more trouble as quickly as they had appeared.

When Father looked around, he realized that they were standing in front of an opening in the fence. Although both sides of the opening might be electrified, they decided to take a chance and made the few steps that brought them to the other side. Then they stopped and took a deep breath, and Father said, "I can't believe it, but we are in Austria." They started to walk toward a small blinking light way ahead of them. When they were at a safe distance from the fence and knew they were no longer in danger, Kato néni said, "We have to find a taxi."

"'Are you crazy, Mother?' I said to her. 'We are in the middle of Burgenland in the fields and that blinking light is probably a farmer's house, and you want a taxi? Even if there was one, where would the money come from to pay for it?' Kato smiled and slowly retrieved some cash hidden between her ample breasts."

They continued to walk slowly and when they reached the source of the light, it was indeed a farmhouse. It was two o'clock in the morning and they discussed whether they should awaken the owner. But as if by magic, the door opened. In a mixture of Austrian and Hungarian, the farmer asked, "What, just the two of you today?" Father tried to tell him about their perilous escape, but the farmer was not interested. "I hear this every night," he said. "I stay up to wait because I know that someone will knock on my door. Is Vienna where you want to go?"

"Yes," Father said. "How can we get there?"

"Do you have any money?" he asked. "If you do, I can call Jacob down the road. He has a car and he will drive you to Vienna, which is only an hour and a half away. If those Hungarian crooks, those border guards, took all of your money, as they often do, I can call the police and they will be happy to bring you to the nearest refugee shelter." They chose Jacob and that is how they arrived at our door at four o'clock that morning.

We are speechless listening to him. Father looks exhausted. He finally stops pacing and sits down. Kato néni is stirring and is almost ready to wake up from her little nap. Mother calls on me to fix the bed in Katika's room. She is away at camp for another week so Father and Kato néni can share her room. Pista helps me pull out the folding bed from behind a curtain in the hallway and put it in Katika's room. I make the beds. It is almost morning now. Everybody is very tired but Mother suggests breakfast. Kato néni speaks—it seems for the first time since she arrived—and says, "Yes, I'm really hungry."

I am dispatched to fetch milk, a couple of rolls, some eggs, and butter from the store around the corner, which opens at six o'clock, because what we have in our small refrigerator is not enough for breakfast for all of us. Mother does not believe in keeping too much food at home anyway. "Just in case," she always says.

"Just in case of what?" I always ask. "We might not come

home" is her standard answer. "Where would we be?" I always think, but I don't ask.

Breakfast is pleasant, with some more talk of their escape. I think they are starting to believe that they are finally really safe. There is some talk about their plan to get to Australia to join my father's sister, Hedi, who got married in Budapest and emigrated with her new husband the year before. Since Father and Kato néni have been relieved of their money, a way has to be found for Hedi to provide them not only with immigration papers but also with sufficient funds to tide them over until they are ready to leave Vienna. Kato néni is sorry to have given up their money. "You don't fight when there is a gun to your head. Although," she continues, "I did consider singing but I was afraid that my voice would uncock the trigger."

I giggle, knowing how strong and compelling my grand-mother's voice can be. Pista too finds her remark humorous. He laughs and asks, "Had you decided to sing, from which of the operas that made you famous would you have sung?" Kato néni smiles, looks happy, says without stopping to think, "Azucena, the strong gypsy woman from Verdi's *Il Trovatore*."

I know the opera well, and I know that Azucena is one of her most famous roles. For some reason I clap, and both Pista and my father clap too as if she had actually given a performance. Only my mother holds out for a second or two, clearly showing that she is not willing to give up her long-standing hostilities with her former mother-in-law. Eventually, she joins in with a pained smile on her face. Kato néni is happy for the recognition she is getting and turns her attention to her breakfast.

When she finishes eating, she leaves the table to take a bath and then go to bed. I show her to Katika's room and explain the intricacies of the ancient hot water system in the bathroom. As soon as we are out of Mother's view, I receive a hug and a number of kisses from my grandmother and then a conspiratorial smile indicating that the strong affection we have for each other will remain private. I am pleased that she sees it that way. After all, neither of us want to upset my mother.

Going back to the other room, I hear my father talking about the substantial amount of money the border guards took. His voice is halting and it sounds like he is ready to cry. "I can't even take you out for coffee," he says, turning to me as I enter the room. I shake my head without saying anything because I am afraid if I speak I am going to cry. I sit down as the conversation continues. Mother takes the lead now and she says, "You can stay here in Katika's room until she comes home from camp in a week, although if you find a good pension nearby you can move earlier. But first we have to get you some clothes. We have to notify your sister, Hedi, in Australia that you arrived safely. You have to ask her for money immediately because you will need it until your visas and tickets arrive. Pista and I will lend you a certain sum so you and Kato can be independent and get around. You will have to learn that Vienna is partially occupied by Russians and which parts of the city you will absolutely have to avoid."

Pista enters the conversation. "Most importantly, you are lucky you have your passports because a new passport is impossible to get from the Hungarian Consulate. They would arrest you for having crossed the border illegally and take you back to Hungary to jail. As soon as possible, you will have to go to the Austrian government offices to apply for confirmation of your refugee status, proof of which you will need to identify yourself anywhere."

Father's thank-you to Mother and Pista is profound and

moving, and like so many times in the last few hours, I can barely stop myself from crying. I try because Mother hates my crying, but today I find it very difficult to keep my tears back. The conversation slows. Right now, everyone is exhausted. Father leaves for his room and a couple of hours of sleep.

I too go to my room worrying because I am still in a state of disgrace and wondering how much and how soon my "sins" will be the subject of Mother's discussions with Father.

CHAPTER FIFTEEN

VIENNA AND ST. PÖLTEN

• 1949 •

FOR THE NEXT FEW days, we are busy getting Father and Kato néni settled with new clothes, new shoes, and other necessities. The sad tale of my "disgrace" is not mentioned. But sometimes Father looks at me and I'm wondering if he knows, especially when he asks, "What is wrong between you and your mother?"

"Nothing," I say, but I know that he knows I am lying.

Mother and I look after Kato néni, while Pista helps Father to get in touch with my Aunt Hedi in Australia. It is not easy to make that phone call. It involves two or three long-distance operators, plus a sixteen-hour time difference. We finally succeed. We find out that Hedi and her new husband, Gyuszi, have already started to work on immigration visas and tickets for a "boat ride." That's what Father calls it—a "boat ride."

"It will feel more like a pleasure cruise," he says to sweeten the prospect of three weeks on a refugee ship. Neither Kato néni nor Father complain; rather, they are happy and looking forward to being "legitimate immigrants" on their way to a new life with the family in Australia.

They move out of our apartment at the end of the week to a nearby pension, but they still spend most of the day with us, for lunch, dinner, and most other activities. Mother is not very happy. She does not have a big problem with my father, but Kato néni gets on her nerves. My grandmother is in her sixties and seems to have no inhibitions. She speaks Hungarian in the grocery store, although they do not understand her. This does not bother her. She points, she takes, she smiles—and manages to get whatever she needs. My mother, on the other hand, who always insists on proper behavior, suffers in her presence, even at home where Kato néni starts to hold court with some Hungarian acquaintances and their friends telling stories, singing songs, and drinking coffee endlessly. Fortunately, Mother is out most of the day working. Pista too works long hours. He has a job as a director with an export-import company, and strangely enough when he comes home, he and my father seem to enjoy each other's company. Pista, the music lover, sings along with Kato néni whenever he can to my mother's great chagrin.

By the weekend, Katika is back from camp and upsets whatever accommodations have been established in the household with her undisciplined and aggressive behavior. Her school in the city starts a week after her return. She will be in second grade and gone from eight o'clock in the morning to one o'clock in the afternoon, five days a week. Mother engages a nanny to pick her up from school and spend the afternoon with her, doing homework, walking, and doing whatever else might keep her out of everybody's hair.

My boarding school in St. Pölten also starts next week. I like my school and had been looking forward to going back after the summer holidays, but that was before my father reentered my life. I enjoy having him here. I enjoy talking with him. I enjoy hearing him call me beautiful names, like "my shining star," "the light of my eyes," "my sweet little girl," and "my one and only love." I also enjoy his patience with my stories.

Every day for the remaining week I'm home, we go for a walk. The Stadtpark, a famous Viennese landmark near our apartment, is still somewhat in ruins and is too close to the Russian zone for us to feel safe. We stroll around the perimeter of the park and visit some other Viennese attractions, like the Burggarten, observing how badly the city is still damaged. The famous Stephansdom, a magnificent cathedral, is in ruins. It is hard to imagine that it will ever be reconstructed to its former glory. But work has started and the scaffolding blocks most of the small streets around it. We walk on the Ringstrasse, where some buildings have already been repaired. Occasionally, a few trees, hardy survivors of the war, are blooming and gracing the sidewalk.

On our walks, my father and I are having serious conversations about life, about philosophy, and of course, about love. "Do you have a boyfriend?" he asks. I feel myself turning beet red. "Of course not," I say.

"Why not?" Father persists.

I don't know how to answer. All of a sudden, I am sure that he has been informed of my unacceptable behavior, and I am so embarrassed I would like the earth to open up and swallow me. But that is not what happens. We are near a bench and Father says, "We are going to sit down. I have heard some stories about your behavior at camp, but now I want to hear the story from you." Then he adds, "I know that you will tell me the truth as you always have." We sit down and for a while I don't know what to say. Then I come out with it. "There was a boy, Peter, that I liked, and with his brother, Wolfgang, we all had a good time until Peter took a girl named Sissy out on his boat, leaving Wolfgang and me behind." At this point I start crying, remembering how awful I felt. Father pulls out a big handkerchief from his pocket, gives it to me to dry my tears, and says, "And what happened then?"

"Wolfgang took me home to their house and told me that I could cry now if I wanted to, and I did. Then he gave me schnapps, saying that I would feel better. But it made me cry even more."

"And then?" asks Father.

I look at him through my tears, and I am angry. "Are you going to torture me like everybody else with questions of *What did he do to you, where did he touch you?*" Father pulls me to him and says, "No, no questions. You can tell me because I am going to believe you. And no matter what he did, I won't think that anything shameful happened, even if he did touch you, even if he did kiss you, even if he did want to be closer to you."

"But Father," I say, "nothing of the sort ever happened. Wolfgang treated me like an older brother would and consoled me about the fact that Peter went off with another girl. Just like you, he gave me a handkerchief and told me it was okay to cry. He said he was sorry that his brother hurt my feelings. That's all that happened and nobody believes me. It is true that I had a second schnapps and got a little bit drunk. Wolfgang was worried that I would be late for lunch and he sent me on my way, although I was a little tipsy."

I stop crying. There is a long silence. Then Father says, "Thank you for telling me the truth. I believe you. And I'm angry, angry at all of the people—the director of the camp, the nuns in your previous school, and especially your mother—for not believing you. I'm angry at them for corrupting your mind with the idea of a sinful body. You are a beautiful young girl turning into a

woman, and you are entitled to your body and to your feelings.
When your time comes, you will be entitled to be kissed and
touched. I want you to remember what I am telling you. Your
body is yours, and you alone are responsible for what you do
with it."

I am confused, but I feel good and I stop crying. When we
get up from the bench, Father gives me a big hug. I give him
back his handkerchief and we continue our walk. The subject is
never discussed again, but I still remember every word.

Meanwhile, living at home with my mother and Katika is
difficult. Pista is nice and funny and I like joking around with
him. The trouble is that Mother does not like laughter—she
does not know how to laugh. "Don't laugh so much," Pista
warns me one time when I giggle at something he said. "You
know your mother does not like it." And she does not.

"Go finish cleaning your room," she says. "I think you forgot
to put the bolster back on your bed."

"No, I didn't," I mutter under my breath. I do not dare to
object. So I go back to my room to check.

"When you finish," Mother yells as I am leaving the room,
"you can take Katika for a walk. She is getting restless."

Still, my father's presence has changed my mother's behavior
quite a bit. She is not as angry as she would normally be. I discuss the situation with my father—I am so happy I can speak to
somebody who does not get angry with me. He tells me to try
to be understanding of my mother's "condition." He calls her
super-nervous and fearful and blames our war experience, although, he says, "She has always, even before the war, had a
difficult character. But remember," he adds, "without her cunning and somewhat devious nature, none of you would be alive."

I do not like what he says. It sounds like he is criticizing my heroic mother. Only I am allowed to do that. But this is a stupid thought because I know that he is right. Her cheating, lying, and stealing, as well as her quick wit and courage, helped us get through. But the more I think about it, the more I realize that my mother's behavior these days is really strange. It does not contribute to the "normal life" that she insists we have to work to have.

It is Sunday and I am going back to the convent in St. Pölten. I am looking forward to seeing some of my classmates from last year and even some of my teachers, in particular Mother Shushinsky, the music teacher. She helps me with a lot of things. She listens patiently to my stories and believes me just like my father. It is strange that I become friendly with a music teacher because, to my great regret, I cannot sing. It was always a disappointment to my family that I cannot carry a tune, in spite of being the granddaughter of an opera singer. Mother Shushinsky spends hours trying to help me overcome my inability without success. I am never able to make it to sing in the choir. Nevertheless, I learn from her how to listen to classical music and how to appreciate quality.

Before Pista drives me back to the convent, I say goodbye to my father with tears in my eyes. I may see him in a month when I go home for the weekend. I can't be sure since as soon as their papers arrive, they will leave for Australia.

Back at the convent, nothing much has changed. All of the girls from last year have returned. The rules are the same as well. They still don't let us take more than one supervised bath a week. We are still expected to study four to six hours a day in the study room. But I'm comfortable here and spend a lot of time with Mother Shushinsky. I tell her about my family situation, about my mother's behavior, her screaming and accusations about situations that happen mostly in her mind, and about Pista's inability to protect me.

Telling my stories to Mother Shushinsky, I become more and more convinced that this is god's way of calling me to leave my family and enter the religious life. I spend long sessions in prayer and I am convinced that my future life is in the convent. Mother Shushinsky is an excellent listener when it comes to hearing about my home life and very understanding of how my family's past history might have affected my mother and brought on her strange behavior. At the same time, she is not as convinced as I am about the validity of my "calling." Every time I bring it up, she tells me that I am too young to have such fervent convictions, and I should put the idea aside until I can make a valid and acceptable decision in maturity. She feels that "my calling" can be interpreted as an escape and advises me to wait and see.

"In my estimation," Mother Shushinsky says, "God created your wonderful large hips for childbearing." Shortly after that conversation, my desire for a saintly life begins to ebb.

That fall, it is announced that there is a possibility for students to spend summer vacation, including studying English, at one of the sister convents in Brighton, England. Two months on the seashore sounds good, even if the domicile is a convent, and the cost is affordable. I am waiting for my Christmas vacation to broach the subject with my mother. Unfortunately, my father and grandmother have already left for Australia. I did not get a chance to say goodbye to them. I know they would have been a supportive influence. I don't know why I am so convinced that my mother would be against my going to England, except for the money. There is always so much fuss made about every penny that is spent that I can't see how she will go for it. Also, it is difficult to get money out of Austria into England, but the convent had made provisions for a reciprocity arrangement. It turns out that this was one time when my mother surprised me. She is in favor of my going and improving my English. She is going to be proud to have a daughter who summers in England. I sign up.

But before that, Christmas vacation is looming and I'm going home. I hate Christmas. I am wondering what unpleasant plans we are going to have this time. Mother has a twisted love for spending New Year's in hotels. It is her fantasy that this is how good "normal Christian families" spend the holiday. This year, we end up in Kitzbühel, which is basically a ski resort. None of us are skiers, though. We spend our days marking time in the hotel or walking around the village, followed by a nap and five o'clock tea in the hotel lobby, consisting of some cakes and biscuits with coffee or tea, card games, reading, and dancing to a band. I am thoroughly bored.

The highlight of the vacation is New Year's Eve, much anticipated by my mother, to show off our beautiful evening clothes. It is a formal affair and usually quite a bit of fun. I am a mature fifteen-year-old, and Pista gets mad at any man who comes near me. Then Mother gets mad at Pista because she wants me to dance. I don't have a lot of fun.

By the time I go back to school in mid-January, I start to prepare for summer camp in England by concentrating on learning more English. I am very excited, and my desire for a saintly life dissipates entirely. I can hardly wait for my summer trip to Brighton.

There are only a few days between the end of the school year and my departure, spent putting together a summer wardrobe, consisting of the prescribed uniform plus a few extra things should the opportunity to wear them arise. I join a group of girls from school and we take a train to Calais, France, which takes a day and a night, and a boat from there to Dover, England. The boat trip across the English Channel is memorable. I have never before seen the sea. Although I have been on a sailboat on a lake, I have never experienced anything like this. For me, it becomes a benchmark because I realize that from here on, I will have to take charge of my life, no matter the circumstances. I cannot rely on my family to help me make decisions. They are just too disturbed, unreasonable, and unrealistic. All they want, they say, is a "normal life." Unfortunately, they don't seem to know what a normal life is, and nor do I. Thinking about being on my own is frightening, but also liberating. By the time we disembark, I feel like this might be my chance for a new and independent beginning.

CHAPTER SIXTEEN

LONDON AND GRADUATION

• 1950–1951 •

WE ARRIVE IN LONDON and spend the night at a convent. The next day we do some sightseeing with the nuns, and then we all take the bus to Brighton. The convent there is on the shore close to the beach. These nuns are not very strict. We have a lot of freedom and a lot of fun. This is new to me. We have only two hours of lessons a day and then are allowed to spend a few hours on the beach, weather permitting.

I am thinking a lot about my home life, and now that I'm away, about my mother. There is never a moment of peace around her. Whatever I say turns into a weapon against me in her mouth. She challenges until you blow up. I am not yet sixteen years old, and I do not want to go back to my mother. I do not want to go back to Austria. I am sitting on the beach plotting how I can manage to stay in England.

The friendly nuns at the convent, particularly a Sister Mary Anne, recommend a convent with a boarding school of good reputation in London. By the end of the summer, we hope my English will have improved enough so I can seriously consider going to school in London for the next couple of years. The nuns arrange an interview with the Mother Superior of the convent at St. Joseph's in Hendon, which is a borough in northern London. They tell me they may be willing to admit me without interviewing my parents. When I go to London to see the Mother Superior, she spends quite a bit of time with me and is inclined to accept me if financial arrangements can be worked out. She would have liked to speak to my family but is willing to forgo a phone interview with my parents because of the language barrier, and she accepts a recommendation from the sisters at St. Pölten.

The next hurdle is finding a way to finance my stay. Monetary restrictions between England and Austria are extremely strict, and you still cannot send money from one country to another in these postwar times. After my mother agrees to my extended stay in England, an exchange of money takes place between my family and some distant relatives in London, Hedi and Irving Miller. They have family in trouble in Vienna who need money. My family has me in London with my need for money. An arrangement is made between the two families to pay each other's bills.

In the fall, I begin my school year in London. St. Joseph's is frequented by daughters of the diplomatic corps and other dignitaries, politicians, and businessmen stationed in the cities. It is one of the few reputable Catholic schools in Protestant England, and it is a huge contrast from the Austrian convent where the school population consisted mostly of "special cases." Here, only twenty or thirty girls in their last two years of classes are boarding at the school. The rest of the student population goes home at four o'clock. Since there are only a few boarders, we receive a lot of attention and supervision from the nuns and a lot of help with our studies. Our living quarters are much more modern than those I was used to in St. Pölten, but a resident nun still shares our dormitory, living in a little cubicle near the entrance door. The windows of the cubicle can be opened so she can hear any and all noise made by the students. Leaving your own cubicle except for short bathroom visits is strictly forbidden. Talking after lights out is another big infraction. The nuns here may be just as strict as the Austrian nuns but they are friendly. I do not fear them. They punish you with a smile and forgive you your mistakes almost instantly.

In spite of what I picked up that summer, I still speak only limited English. It is decided by the headmistress and my adviser that I be entered at a lower grade than my age group to give me a chance to develop my language skills. But by Christmas my English fluency has vastly improved, and I am allowed to join my age-appropriate class, the Fifth Form, so that at the end of the year I too will receive my School Leaving Certificate like the other girls my age.

I spend my first Christmas vacation in the convent with two other girls whose parents are on diplomatic missions abroad. I have a lot of time to study and to start to think about how to advance my studies in the coming year. I find out that obtaining my School Leaving Certificate is not enough for entering a British college. For that, you need to pass an entrance examination from the particular college that you want to attend. I'm not sure yet what I am going to study, but I know that I want to go to college. I get information from Oxford, Cambridge, and the University of London with the requirements of their college entrance examinations. I will barely qualify for their age requirement. Most students take an additional year of classes to prepare to take the exam when they are around eighteen, but I will be just sixteen and a half. Nevertheless, I decide to take a chance and register for all three exams. Fortunately, they are on different days of the same month. I realize that I cannot expect the approval of my school to do the extra work and decide to do my studying in a safe place, namely at night under the blanket. The Millers, the family paying my bills, help me get the necessary study material, a flashlight and batteries, and some money for registration and travel. I begin my extra studies hoping that I will pass at least one exam.

Soon, the nuns have figured out what I am doing, and in spite of my fears, they do not stop me and reluctantly wish me well. They allow me time off to take the exams and I pass all three, barely. At the end of the school year, I also receive my School Leaving Certificate from St. Joseph's with distinctions in mathematics, German, and literature.

I return home for the summer intending to go back to England in the fall to begin college. I haven't quite decided which college I want to go to, but soon after I arrive, Mother informs me that we don't have enough money for me to go to school away from home. There have been major changes while I was away as a result of serious business reversals the year before. We are now living in a small apartment in a cheap residential suburb as our big apartment in the city is rented out. Mother is no longer involved with the clothing factory. Although it employed more than two hundred people, it was closed down because of a foreign currency infraction. Apparently, this was a major scandal in the city. It was on the front pages of the newspapers, with Mother's picture and a story about her involvement. Mother refuses to answer my inquiries about what actually happened and tells me to accept the new circumstances without questions. I want to find out more about the story, but neither Mother nor Pista are willing to talk.

Soon after I arrive back in Vienna, I receive a message from

Hippich, the former manager of the factory. When I lived in Vienna, she was my friend and often commiserated with me when Mother treated me badly in front of her. She was very funny and nice and we usually had a good time. She asks me to have lunch and pours her heart out about the events of the past year.

Hippich blames Mother and Pista for ruining the business. Mother spent way too much money traveling to Paris for fashion ideas with a new, much younger business partner. It was alleged that the partner brought in large sums of money for expansion, but according to Hippich, he was laundering illegal funds. Pista should have known since he was the one taking care of the company's finances. Hippich calls Mother many ugly names. She also tells me that Sandor Lehr was in love with my mother when she first started to work for him and that they had an affair. He was inconsolable when she took this younger man into the business as a partner and a lover. Sandor was left with no livelihood when the business went under. He was despondent and committed suicide, jumping out of a window into a courtyard.

Hippich had worked for Sandor for more than thirty years managing the business and was considered part of the family. No wonder her anger is palpable. Although the new business partner was jailed for ten years, Hippich was left without a job and a secure old age. For the first time, I realize that my mother's irresponsible actions and erratic behavior can no longer be excused as merely shell shock from the war. In contrast to my usual reaction when somebody attacks my mother, in this case I cannot defend her. I realize that it is not me alone who is being hurt by her actions. For the first time I know that her craziness affects everyone. On the way home from lunch, I decide not to bring up the subject with Mother and Pista. I go straight to my room and do not mention my meeting with Hippich.

Mother and Pista were happy to see me when I first came home from England. It didn't last long. I have gained some weight while away, which is a constant embarrassment to my slim mother. She puts a lock on the refrigerator. Although I play a lot of tennis and start to lose a few kilos, still the fridge stays locked. Mother is in a terrible mood, all of the time complaining about the loss of her business. She sits at the kitchen table and stares into space.

Pista is very war-damaged and he seems to be getting worse. He screams during his nightmares in the middle of many nights. He is often agitated and compulsive. He prepares towers of little chocolate squares on his night table and eats them one by one in bed while he is reading. If he runs out of them before he is ready to stop reading, he yells for more chocolates loud enough so that I can hear him and run to get them. He is neurotic and he loses his temper easily for obscure reasons.

It is not a "normal life."

I have been away for a while and have learned that not all people behave like my family does. I don't know how I am going to cope with living at home, since I am not going back to England. According to the Austrian system, I am too young for university.

I still have some religion left in me, so I go to Mass at the church down the street and join the youth group. The leader is a priest in his early thirties and very good-looking. His name is Pater Sint. I soon discover that he has an eye for me. He is looking at me all of the time. He tries to stand next to me as often as possible, and I don't mind at all. I enjoy his attention.

Later in the summer, my group and several chaperones go

on an excursion mountain climbing. Pater Sint is the leader. It is undeniable throughout the weekend that there is a very strong attraction between us. I cannot concentrate on anything but him when he is near me. Finally, he asks me to take a walk with him and we talk.

"I'm in love with you," says Pater Sint. When I hear his words, I start to shake. I am elated and embarrassed. I have had an occasional boyfriend, but I've never been in love like this before. My convent life has not allowed me the opportunity to meet many boys—not that this can be called a typical dating situation.

"I'm in love with you too," I say, "but I don't know what to do with it." His answer astonishes and delights me.

"I'm going to leave the priesthood," he says, "as soon as we get back to Vienna. I'll marry you."

I am confused and both happy and disturbed. We make arrangements. We agree to elope and leave Vienna. The plan is to meet at the train station a few days later, travel to Salzburg to stay with his relatives, and get married.

At the appointed time I go to the train station. When I see him through the window of the train compartment, he is still wearing a collar. I know that he has made a decision, and I too have come to the right decision. I am not going to do it. I'm not going to elope. I stop under the window and tell him I can't marry him. It is the hardest thing I ever had to do, but I could not face the responsibility of being the cause of him leaving the priesthood. I also believe that I am too young to get married to a man in his thirties.

Now that I am not going back to England and not getting married, I have to find out how my English exams translate into the Austrian system. It turns out that I have more than enough qualifications to enter any program at the university level except medicine, because I have never taken Latin as a subject. There is a lot of discussion about what occupation I should go for. My choice is architecture. I am always preoccupied with beautifying places and making them more functional. But Mother is against it. She wants me to go into medicine and her argument holds true, as painful as it is to hear.

"If you are a good doctor, you can save lives and help people," she says. "No one will care if you are of Jewish origin, even if they find out." I am not sure if I agree with her but I think that she may have a point.

Pista's job as director of Oestawa pays well, and we can afford to move back to our apartment in the center of the city. My mother expresses doubt and fear about his ability to keep the job and do well, so she decides to go to the office with him every day. It's hard to imagine what she does there all day. Her paranoia manifests itself in worrying that Pista will spend money on Katika or even me or just hide money behind her back. His business is with foreign dignitaries and soon he starts doing very well. How does Pista feel about her going to work with him? I do not know and it does not matter because Pista will not fight with her directly. Instead, he blows up suddenly at home, usually about something unimportant. He explodes in anger in a way that is frightening. It comes fast and it is scary but it does not last too long.

I am often in the middle of their arguments. Mother will attack me with something untrue and unjust, and Pista will come to my defense. When Pista is nice to me, Mother gets angry. Only Katika, who is now nine years old and going to the American school, is allowed to answer back. She is also allowed to be very mean to Mother. She gets away with it. Mother cannot control her. She misbehaves during our lunches at restaurants all of the time. After lunch, nanny takes Katika for a walk and Mother goes back to the office with Pista.

I register for a qualifying one-year course in textile engineering, to pass my time while I wait for my acceptance at medical school after I turn eighteen and pass a test in Latin. I am the youngest in the class and I have no experience in the field. The course is very difficult for me. I am not prepared for this kind of technical education. There are a lot of young men between the ages of twenty-five and thirty who already have other degrees and a lot of professional experience. This is a serious graduate course. It entitles you to call yourself an engineer. Thankfully, most of the students recognize my inexperience and help and support me through the difficulties of this training.

One of the young men in my class is called Rolf Driessen. He is twenty-eight with a graduate degree in commerce and wants to specialize in the textile industry. He is tall, blond, and good-looking and undeniably interested in me. He invites me out for lunch. Our conversation is interesting and I am impressed that he treats me as an equal, in spite of our age difference. We discuss some serious subjects of interest, including literature and music. We go out a couple of times and I fall in love with him as he does with me. We discuss our age difference, which we feel is not that significant, and our divergent background, which is substantial. We feel confident that none of that matters. He treats me with respect and love. Soon, the relationship becomes physical.

It doesn't take long for Mother to become suspicious, both of my frequent absences and my smiling face. She starts to investigate my whereabouts. One time, she and Pista follow me in the car when I go to Rolf's apartment. I know nothing about that until one day Rolf sits me down for a serious conversation. He tells me that I am too young and we cannot overcome our difficulties. We are not meant for each other. I try to question him.

"Why did you not ask me how I feel?" I ask. He says his mind is made up. "I love you dearly, but the affair is over."

I do not understand. The pain is blinding me. By the time I get home, I decide to hide my anger, disappointment, and suspicion and not talk about it.

Eventually, it becomes obvious that Mother had something to do with this. A few days later, she asks, "Have you seen Rolf?"

"I'm not seeing Rolf anymore. I will never see him again."

I tell her what happened and her reaction is truly astonishing.

"I saved you from a big mistake," she says. "I went to see Rolf and told him you are too young and too immature to be involved in a serious affair. I also told him that I have forbidden you to see him again."

I cry. It is so unfair, but there is nothing I can do about it. I feel isolated and have no one to talk to. I live as a Catholic girl in a Catholic society. I'm young. I'm not married and I am not supposed to have an affair. To confront my mother would be from a position of weakness, shame, and guilt.

I have a difficult time getting over my pain and disappointment. I try my best to hide what happened and how I feel from my classmates. At the graduation from textile engineering school, I receive a prize for working the hardest and advancing the farthest. When I get my certificate, the loudest applause comes from Rolf. But it no longer matters.

One day, Mother informs me that we are having a visitor for coffee. To my great surprise, Rolf walks in the door. He seems familiar with Mother and Pista and greets me like an old friend. I don't know what to make of it. But then Mother explains that he and Pista are doing business together. After that, his visits are quite frequent. Rolf goes out to eat with us as well. He is very nice to me, acting as if I were his younger sister. Rolf is well versed in Austrian business practices and he seems to be helping Pista in his position with Oestawa. He fits in to the family situation like the older brother he is not. Sometimes I think Rolf is hanging around waiting for me to get older, but that's not the case. After a while, I realize that his big love is my mother.

CHAPTER SEVENTEEN

VIENNA

• 1952–1953 •

IT IS MY FIRST year of medical school at the University of Vienna, and I am slowly learning my way around. I become friends with a group: Wolf, Dennis, John, Reginald, and another Erika. They are all Austrian and come from various parts of the country, sons of good established Austrian families and successful professionals. Only Erika is different, an illegitimate child of a working woman, but it does not seem to matter as she is highly educated and of exceptional intelligence. And she is also good fun. We all study together and go out together and become great friends. I think we all are contemporary, liberal intellectuals, sharing common goals and helping each other to cope with the pressures of our academic lives. We develop intense and support- ive relationships. I'm starting to belong somewhere for the first time in my life. This is particularly important and satisfying to me. Until I started medical school at the age of eighteen, I had attended eight different schools, in three different languages, in three countries. My background as a Hidden Child survivor, a displaced person, and a Catholic girl did not leave room to con- nect or to form attachments.

It is postwar Austria, anti-Semitism is a fact of life, and I carefully guard the secret of my family's history. I am recognized as a refugee of the Communist takeover of Hungary. My credentials as a Christian include an education in convent schools and participation in church-related social activities. My origins are never questioned by my friends, and I am accepted as a well brought-up Catholic girl. The year passes fast with a lot of study and a lot of good times and success.

In my second year, I no longer need to prove myself. Passing my first-year exams with high honors has earned me a place among this elite group of bright and accomplished students. I am a fully accepted member of the group. We spend eight or ten hours a day together, having been assigned our first dissecting exercises in the lab. It is mostly manual labor and it leaves us a lot of time to talk about books, art, philosophy, and our ambitions in life.

But today is a new day. The weather is pleasant for late fall. It is clear and quite balmy, with no wind, which is unusual for this time of year. I live twenty minutes' walk from the lab, where I am heading this morning. I usually enjoy the brisk walk, but this particular morning I feel apprehensive and cannot shake a sense of foreboding. As I approach the school my thoughts turn to the conversation that took place the day before. The subject was politics. Austria is still in a lot of denial about the events of World War II. During the discussion, I was surprised by the attitude of my friends and frightened by the direction the conversation was taking. I listened quietly and remained silent. The possibility of a continued discussion of the subject today fills me with anxiety and apprehension. If necessary, I am prepared to spend the next six hours in the lab in silence.

Shortly after we start to work, as I feared, the conversation picks up where it left off the day before. I sit in stunned silence as my very intelligent, sophisticated friends paint a picture of Austria as the victim of Nazi aggression. They consider the Anschluss to be a German military invasion and regard Austria's participation in the war and acceptance of Nazi ideology as certainly not voluntary. To my horror, the next subject of discussion is a debate about concentration camps. They feel that the existence of the camps cannot be reasonably denied, but their role must have been to help the war effort. They think that the goal of exterminating the Jewish people is not only an exaggeration but a lie. Nobody in Austria, not the government and certainly not their own families or friends, would have cooperated. "Unimaginable," says one of my friends, "that any of our parents could ever have participated or sanctioned the alleged atrocities involved in the persecution and extermination of the Jews. Under no circumstances could that have found support from self-respecting Austrian citizens."

I am frozen into a state of disbelief, disgust, and fear. I am terrified to open my mouth, knowing that I will give myself away as Jewish, and yet my indignation at their ignorance and denial becomes explosive. The ashes of my cousins, aunts, and uncles gassed at Auschwitz are demanding that I speak.

I stand up and say in a loud clear voice, "Listen to me!" The room is becoming silent as eighty people turn toward me. "I want to tell you what it is like to be Jewish and to have lost sixteen members of my family through extermination in the gas chambers of the concentration camps you do not believe existed!" I hesitate for a moment as fear constricts my throat. I see my friends staring at me in astonishment, but I continue. "Those of us who survived," I say, "did so by denying our Jewishness, using fake papers, hiding in caves, attics, and cellars. I learned to lie and cheat and steal to save my life. I listen to you pretend that Austria is blameless. It is a historical fact that the Anschluss was willingly accepted and embraced by the government of Austria, by its people, and by the Austrian Army. Austria was a willing ally in the German effort to exterminate Jews in order to keep the Aryan race *Judenfrei* [free of Jews]. You will have to face the fact of the participation of your country and the Austrian people in the atrocities committed against Jews. If you perpetuate the denial of the truth, you are paving the way for the possibility of the Holocaust repeating itself. And this is unacceptable."

I stop speaking. The room is silent. Nobody moves. As I turn to make my exit, silence accompanies me to the door. I can feel imaginary scalpels being thrown at my back. I don't know what gave me the strength to stand up and express my feelings in spite of the certainty that I will be condemned and ostracized. Whatever the consequences at that moment, I feel relieved and liberated.

The catharsis manifests itself in my stomach with serious rumblings and retching. I head for the bathroom, hoping to reach it in time. I become violently ill and vomit for what seems like a long time. When I leave the bathroom, I feel a reassuring hand on my shoulder. It is the security guard at the door to the lab whom I had never spoken to before except to say "good morning.

"I heard every word," he says in his distinctly Viennese accent, "and it is high time someone had the courage to speak the truth!"

This reassurance calms me for the walk home. I am not planning to tell my mother what happened, but as soon as I open the door, she screams at me. "What is wrong? You seem like you have seen a ghost." I do tell her what I did, and her violent reaction brings home the probable consequences of my action. "You idiot, you moron! You just killed your future! You will see. You will have no more friends and your professors will never let you pass another exam. Don't you know they're all anti-Semites? You should never have let them find out that you're Jewish."

I am physically ill for two days and stay home and worry constantly about the reaction to my disclosure. I finally muster the courage to go back to the lab, back to my friends. But they are no longer there. My dearest and best Austrian friends have checked out from my table, checked out of my study group, and checked out of my life. For the next two years I study alone. I sit in the library alone, and when I walk into our favorite coffeehouse, I occupy a table all by myself. I try to say hello, but no one ever responds. I feel as if I have a contagious, possibly fatal disease.

A few months after my disclosure, I have my first major oral exam. It is held on the stage of a large auditorium, before a professor and several members of the faculty. The auditorium is usually quite empty during orals. It is not customary to listen to fellow students' failures or triumphs. Except for one's best friends, no one shows up on these occasions. But not this time, not at my exam—the seats are filled to the rafters with students who I think have come to witness my downfall. Although I am very well prepared, after I hear the first question I look out into the audience and freeze. My mind goes blank, and I think of my mother's prophecy. I am going to fail. I will never make it. I think that my professor is an anti-Semite. I might as well walk out right now. But to my surprise, the professor recognizes my predicament. He gently takes me by the arm, turns me around so that I am no longer facing the audience, and repeats the question. I answer that question and all that follow without fault.

My grade for the exam is the highest possible, and at the end of the semester, I receive a distinction for my second year's work.

THE MAIN MEAL OF the day is lunch, but Mother never cooks. She insists that we all meet at an affordable restaurant near the university. I'm expected to join at the appointed place at the appointed time, which I have to fit into my schedule or otherwise I go hungry. There is not much to eat at the apartment, and even if there was food, I cannot go home anyway. Mother does not want any of us to enter the apartment alone. She is afraid of who might be there waiting for us. At the end of Pista's workday, we meet at the nearby coffeehouse and enter the apartment in unison. This was only one of Mother's more obvious manifestations of her deteriorating mental state—her paranoia.

After a while when Pista's job seems really secure, it is decided that we can have lunch at home. As Mother says, "We will try to have a normal life." The first step toward that goal is to engage a housekeeper. Her job is not just to clean but also to cook. She is supposed to cook one good meal a day that we will have in the early hours of the afternoon at home. The housekeeper, Hilda, is pretty good, or at least I think so. She cleans and cooks and is generally quite jolly. I like her. One afternoon she is going to serve some fish stew, which is a dish that I do not like. When she tells me what we are going to have, I tell her I won't eat it. Good-natured as she is, she brings in the fish stew and a dish with sausage salad for me.

Mother is appalled. "How dare you indulge her fancy!"

Pista is hungry and happy with the fish stew so he starts to eat and tells Mother to let it go for once.

For unknown reasons, I wake up with diarrhea the next morning. I am convinced that it has nothing to do with the sausage salad but I can't convince Mother. The incident turns into a cause célèbre. Mother insists that Pista immediately fire Hilda because Mother is afraid of her. "She tried to poison Erika. She knows Erika is in the third year of medical school and can diagnose Hilda as the crazy woman she is." There is no way to convince Mother of her delusion.

I am very upset. Although it is often clear that Mother's mental health is in bad shape, it has not been as clear to me before as it is now. Pista plays his usual role of appeaser. He will say, "Let her be. Don't upset her. Don't tell her how wrong she is." He fires Hilda, and the few weeks of good meals are over.

That night when we all come home in unison, I make up my mind to move out but this lasts only a few weeks before I surrender. Mother does not support me, even with one penny. I take a job to support myself as a night waitress from ten o'clock at night until two o'clock in the morning, but it is too exhausting. I develop bronchitis and pneumonia. I have to see a doctor, go on medication, and move back home. The craziness continues.

"You will not be ready on time," yells my mother from the other room one morning.

Today I decide not to answer with some provocative remark, although I very often do. I have a whole repertoire of answers to give her because her *You will not be ready* or *Are you ready yet?* or *Hurry up, it's late* are standard early morning remarks of hers, solely for the purpose of yelling and, in particular, yelling at me. At this early hour of the morning, Pista is still asleep and Katika is away at boarding school. I am the only one to feel the bait of her anger, unprovoked and undeserved.

Why is she yelling? Why is she so sure I will be late? My first class at the university starts at seven thirty. I am usually ready, showered and dressed by six thirty, and we live only twenty minutes away. I am ready now, but another part of the morning ritual still has to be enacted. I have to go downstairs to the bakery to buy our daily quota of fresh rolls and milk for the innumerable coffees my mother drinks and serves in her "salon" to her customers. She now makes custom clothes for clients. I take the money she gives me and run downstairs. The bakery is just around the corner, and I get what I get every day—a quart of milk, four rolls, and ten dekagrams of butter.

She waits for me at the door and takes the bag and the milk and holds out her other hand for the change. She looks at the few pennies I give her and the daily exchange, predictable and ugly, starts right then.

"Where is the rest of the money?" she asks.

"What rest? That's all she gave me back from the bill you gave me."

"That is impossible," says Mother. Her voice is high-pitched and approaching its customary yelling mode. "There is some money missing."

"That is impossible," I say and turn my back to leave.

"You are a liar and a thief," she screams.

By the time her voice reaches its highest pitch, I am down the stairs and on the way to school, merrily clutching my pocket, knowing that like on most other days, my cigarette money for today is safe.

CHAPTER EIGHTEEN

VIENNA

• 1954–1955 •

MOTHER SNARLS WHEN SHE looks at me as she opens the door when I come home. "Look at you," she says. "You look disgusting, crumpled, dirty."

"Mother," I say as I try to defend myself, "I just finished a four-hour shift at the hospital and two hours at the library. You are right. I am crumpled, dirty, and tired, and I have another two hours of studying to do."

I go to my room and open my book of notes. Maybe ten or fifteen minutes pass before she barges in without knocking, picks up my cardigan parked on a chair, and starts yelling, "You're so messy. Why don't you put your sweater away when you take it off? Will you ever learn how to be neat?"

I try not to respond. I try to stay calm and detached. I try, but I do not succeed. I come back at her with what seems like an appropriate answer in the form of a question. "Have you tried to open the closet door in your bedroom lately? There are dirty clothes mixed with clean, sweaters, underwear, cardigans, all crumbled, mixed together and shuffled into small shelves."

I am lucky today. She does not yell or scream at me, as she

often does, but turns around and leaves the room, mumbling audibly about my "swollen head." That's her catchphrase for what she considers either right or wrong with me—my education (put down or praised), my intelligence (certainly not from my father), my friends (not one of them is Jewish), my looks (too heavy), and whatever else she can think of at that moment.

Paranoia manifests in her in several ways. She is convinced that everybody cheats her—sometimes in big ways and sometimes in small. She buys five yards of fabric but gets only four and three quarters, or ten grams of butter is only nine and a half. She pays our rent with cash. There are monthly scenes about a missing hundred or two shillings—she swears she gave it to them, and they swear she did not. More importantly, she gets into trouble, even with the law, suing everybody she has a dispute with, however small or big. She has several open court cases with former customers, neighbors, and stores. At one point she wants the court to call me as a witness in one of her cases, but I refuse because I would have had to lie. Mother does not speak to me for several weeks after that, loses the case and many others, and becomes increasingly more anxious and paranoid.

Pista sometimes tries to help in the confrontations between Mother and me. I wish he would step in more strongly, like he does with Katika, and protect me. But whenever he tries, he is relentlessly reminded, "Erika is not your daughter. Keep out of this. She is none of your business. I am handling it and I do not need any help."

I try to stay away from the apartment as much as possible and concentrate on my studies. By now, my Jewishness is a well-known fact. Slowly, in this my third year of med school, new connections and new possibilities open up.

One day, while registering for my next exam, an older man

turns to me and says, "Me, too old, but you, too young." He is very friendly and his smile is more like a laugh. "Coffee, young lady?" he says. Sensing my reluctance, he adds his qualification. "A veteran, finally returning to university, school of dentistry." Somewhat reassured, I accept his invitation.

His name is Herbert. "I am thirty-three," he tells me, "but having spent several years on the Russian front with the Austrian Army fighting on the side of the Germans makes me feel much older."

I'm wondering why he seems to be interested in me. Does he know I'm Jewish? Strangely, I do not feel intimidated by him or his history. I feel his kindness. He is genuine.

Slowly, I find out more about his family—prominent, aristocratic Austrians and very wealthy. They were open supporters of Hitler and the Anschluss, unashamed anti-Semites who sacrificed their oldest son, Herbert's brother, to the cause. The brother joined Hitler's Navy and died a "hero" as a U-boat commandant. The family's worship of their dead hero was excessive. When Herbert came home from the Russian front for his brother's memorial, he was expected to marry his late brother's pregnant girlfriend, which he did. Herbert's marriage is now on the rocks, but he and his wife still live together with the child at his parents' home. He is disillusioned and estranged from all of them but still financially dependent until he can establish his dental practice.

Against all odds, we fall passionately in love. If he ever sympathized with Nazi ideology before the war, he came back from military service disillusioned and aware of Germany's role in the persecution and extermination of the Jewish people. He is one of those Austrians who believe there were concentration camps, ghettos, executions, and killings. He is appalled at his parents' continuing acceptance of Nazi doctrine—the right of the master race to dominate the world. He is a man of integrity and honesty. But Herbert's most redeeming characteristic is his sense of humor. Actually, it is more wit than humor. After my year of isolation by classmates, friends, and other people who rejected my Jewishness, being involved with a former Nazi who cherishes my Jewishness is a revelation.

For a short while we believe that our love will conquer all. Herbert divorces his wife and we move in together. To my astonishment, my mother accepts Herbert. She is very impressed with his family's name, his manners, and his education because he went to the best schools. She is very impressed that he married his late brother's girlfriend. There is no objection when I move out of our house and in with him, which shocks me. She has always preached that a woman must live at home with her family until marriage. I am surprised. I didn't expect Mother to feel as comfortable with Herbert as she eventually does.

It does not take long to find out that we are breaking the laws of society around us. Postwar or not, Jews like me are not acceptable in any of Herbert's circles. His parents cut his financial support to a bare minimum, refusing to support "the Jewess." His former friends are mostly critical of his actions and no longer wish to socialize with us. I did not have any Jewish friends of my own before I met Herbert, and certainly not now, living with him. My isolation continues, but now it involves both of us.

Working toward our degrees, we both keep very busy and become more and more miserable. Suddenly one night, I ask Herbert, "Are you happy?" His *no* comes so swiftly that it surprises me, although I more or less expected it.

"I miss the kid," he says. "She won't let me see him for fear of dishonoring his father. I also miss my parents, even if their attitudes are unacceptable to me. I miss my friends, who thought I was a hero marrying my brother's pregnant fiancée to give the child a name but cannot accept that I have a Jewish girlfriend. I am a displaced person."

It surprises me to hear him use that expression, the one that describes my status as a refugee from the Communist takeover of Hungary. In that moment we both know that unless we move to an uninhibited island, our beautiful relationship will not survive. Our subsequent split is sad and painful but without hard feelings, and we remain friends.

After spending some more months alone, my attention is caught by a group of Israeli students. All were born in Palestine. After the establishment of the state of Israel, they had to spend time in the army and developed a strong sense of patriotism. They are at the university on scholarship and they are ambitious. They attend every lecture, making the most of their opportunity, but they keep very much to themselves. I decide to make an effort to get to know them better, now that I'm Jewish. My tentative moves to socialize with them are categorically rebuffed.

"What do you want from us?" says the leader of their group. I ask them to sit down and give me a chance to explain my quest for identity and belonging, but I do not find sympathetic ears. "Your kind of Jews are not wanted in Israel," he says. I ask for an explanation, and they give me one. "You converted. Good, proud Jews don't do that. More importantly, you did not fight. Why did you allow yourselves to be slaughtered like sheep? Why were you too timid and frightened, willing to be victimized? You are not the kind of people we want to build our Israeli society on. You will not fight for the survival of our state. You would probably allow yourself to be killed. That is not the kind of person who will make Israel strong."

That is the strongest rebuff I have ever received from any person or any group. Judging by their rough manners and insensitive words, I doubt if I ever really wanted to be part of their group. "You don't understand what Jewish life was like in Europe," I tell them. "Nor do you see the differences between our culture and yours." But they fail to recognize my efforts. They are not interested. After my painful experience with Herbert, I find this rejection very disturbing. I am not sure whether I will ever belong anywhere—to a religion, a relationship, or a doctrine. I decide instead to put all of my energy into my studies.

This third year is the hardest year of my studies—lectures, major exams, and several hours of hospital duties a week. My isolation continues and I spend most of my time alone. Being at home is the worst. I recognize that Mother's antics have reached major pathological proportions and are signs of mental illness. She accuses everybody of crimes that have never been committed. Often, I sit alone in my favorite coffeehouse to study, sipping for hours on one cup of coffee.

I become friendly with a group of veterans—Kurt, Fritz, and Maiwie—who frequent my coffeehouse. They got their medical degrees on veterans' bills. They are considerably older than I am. Kurt has become a doctor, but he is not interested in practicing medicine. He has political leanings and does not keep it a secret. Both he and Fritz are dedicated socialists who live and think politics. Kurt is big and boisterous, the loudest and the leader of the group. He organizes hospital staff and laborers and whoever else will listen to his speeches. Fritz is his chief lieutenant. Maiwie is a doctor too but without political interests. (Everybody calls him Maiwie, from his family name of Maiwald, but I find out later that he too is named Herbert.)

They soon realize how lonely my Jewishness has made me

and take me up as a "cause," keeping me company. Or maybe their friendliness has something to do with the fact that Maiwie is interested in me. He comes from a poor background. The apartment where he grew up is a walk-up on the outskirts of Vienna. His attachment to his friends dates back to serving in the war. Their common experience has made them devoted to each other forever.

Maiwie is soft-spoken and adores me. There are no serious issues between us. Dating him becomes a new and very satisfying experience. He calls me lovely, endearing names. Most of our conversations are very positive. His loyal friends become my friends as well, and as I am a good many years younger, they take some big brotherly interest in my well-being.

"Where is the old guy?" Kurt asks one day when I arrive at the coffeehouse without Maiwie.

"He is cleaning some stores in the neighborhood, trying to make some money. We don't even have cigarette money anymore, and my mother has not been in a giving mood."

Kurt pulls a few shillings from his pocket and puts them on my side of the table. Fritz, sitting next to him, doubles it, and both Maiwie and I are able to smoke cigarettes for a while.

Maiwie works long hours at the university hospital to get his specialty training, but the pay is lousy. It is difficult to have an intimate relationship since we both live at home and we are both poor. We end up making love mostly on an obstetrician's table after Maiwie takes a job cleaning offices for doctors.

Mother seems reconciled to my relationship with Maiwie. His kind and mild manners, relentless friendliness, and obvious infatuation with me convince her that I am safe. After about a year, Maiwie starts to talk marriage and children. I don't want that now—later maybe, but not yet, not now. I want a career. I don't want a relationship that feels as safe, secure, and predictable as life with Maiwie promises to be. Serious excitement and danger have been part of my life for too long. At times I even miss the sound of sirens signaling the approaching bombardments that were a constant in my childhood. I feel bad about breaking up with Maiwie but nevertheless initiate the end of the relationship.

CHAPTER NINETEEN

VIENNA

• 1956 •

I AM AN INTERN at Vienna University Hospital and have a boyfriend named Adolf. He is a psychologist and an intern at the same hospital. He is very bright and very attractive. We are crazy about each other although very busy in our respective careers.

I am living at home and I am quite unhappy. Lately, Mother's mental state has deteriorated even more. She is as cunning and scheming as she ever was during the war, but it seems to me that at that time it served our survival well. Life at home now consists of a succession of fights of varying intensity without resolution. She has also started to drink, at times losing sight of reality. She maintains that I chose Adolf as my boyfriend only to torture her because he has the same name as Hitler. This reminds her of the war and robs her of sleep.

The start of the Hungarian Revolution in October 1956 is a welcome distraction from my untenable situation. The uprising in Hungary against the continuing Russian occupation has changed our daily lives. We organize to help the stream of refugees into Austria as best we can. Everybody is astonished and elated that a little country like Hungary would rebel against the might of the Communist empire. The brave fighters, the gains they made, and the subsequent influx of refugees into Austria make headlines, not only in Vienna but around the Western world. The sentiments evoked results in unprecedented material help and offers of free immigration to many countries. We are all given time off from our jobs to participate in the rescue efforts. Adolf and I drive a truck to the border every day, about two hours from the city, where we pick up exhausted but exuberant refugees as they climb across the loosened, no longer electrified wires or crawl through the mud under the fence. When our truck is full, we deliver them to the city to hastily assembled refugee centers.

One day I come home exhausted. Mother is waiting for me in the front hall. This is unusual as she normally inhabits the living room and does not get up to greet me. But the French doors leading to the living room, which are usually open, are closed. I wonder for a second who might be in there before a barrage of words from her informs me that I look disgusting and have to clean up before entering the living room to meet our visitor. "Make sure," she says, "to change your clothes, comb your hair, and make yourself presentable."

I understand that I look a sight. Besides the bronchitis that I have had for more than two weeks, I have not eaten properly all day, I have a rash on my face, my hair is hanging in unwashed strands, my clothes are dirty, and there is dried earth slowly falling off my shoes. "Who is our visitor?" I ask. She keeps on repeating, "Go and clean up."

Suddenly, uncontrollable anger grips me. What does she want from me? She doesn't ask how I am, if I had fever in the morning, or how I spent my day helping the refugees. I look at her in defiance and scream as loudly as my bronchitis will allow, "If I am not good enough to meet whoever is in there the way I am, they can leave." I quickly push the door open. Mother looks frightened as she watches me walk in and survey the scene. Pista is sitting in the armchair closest to me, a serving table with coffee and cakes is between him and a rotund, youngish gentleman sitting in the other armchair. He is dressed formally in a navy suit and striped shirt, sweating and visibly uncomfortable. First, he just looks at me and seems a bit astonished, but then he gets up, extends a hand to shake mine, and with a big smile says, "It is an honor and privilege to finally meet you." Suddenly, I get it. The "finally meet you" gives it away. He must be that very successful son of a cousin's cousin on my mother's side now living in Canada whom my mother has been saying I must meet one day.

I realize she must have been plotting this for a long time. She has taken up correspondence with relatives she found in Montreal. That is not so unusual. Relatives and friends were still finding each other, even by coincidence, in the aftermath of World War II. But this son of a cousin's cousin, Tom, has been mentioned more than once. "We'll have to meet him and his family one day," Mother always says. But now, here he is sitting in my living room waiting to meet me, assuming, I think, that I have been waiting to meet him too.

I sit down on the sofa, dropping dried mud on the carpet, knowing that my life with Mother will become even more impossible if I don't show at least some civility toward her "find" for me. She has been actively engaged in her search for a husband for me for the past few years, an almost impossible endeavor under the circumstances. We have remained Catholics, "forever" according to her, never to return to Judaism. It is impossible to have a rational conversation with her about the subject. Often, I have asked, "Who do you think I could go out with and who do you think will want to marry me?" The answer is obsessively the same: "A converted Jew like you, somebody who will understand that I do not wish your children, my grandchildren, to ever go through the same persecutions or experience anti-Semitism firsthand like we did." It has never occurred to her to tell me where to find a suitable person like that.

Recently, she has become more and more irrational and has disapproved of any and all of my dates who were Christians, maintaining that we can never be sure if their relatives possibly killed some of the dead in our family. "My own father," she says, "is turning in his grave every time you go out with one of them." Having dated a Jewish boy once, I knew that that did not work either. His family had wanted me to officially return to Judaism. "Over my dead body," said my mother. Then she asked him to convert to Catholicism if he wanted to marry me or she would object. That was the end of that relationship. I know how sick this way of thinking is on her part, but there is little I can do.

So I am sitting in the living room realizing that according to my mother, this gentleman, Tom, sitting across from me is supposed to be my future husband. I am angry and defiant, and I will have none of it. He is asking me politely to tell him about my day with the refugees, and I describe the circumstances, possibly making them sound even worse than they actually are. He tells me that he is a political scientist, besides being a successful businessman, and teaches at Sir George Williams University in Montreal. I try to be unresponsive because I would really like to get rid of him, but he doesn't give up. He finally tells me that he wants to come on my truck tomorrow and go to the border with me. I say that is impossible as he would take up too much room at the expense of a refugee.

"Oh, I wouldn't want to do that," he says. "Have someone

else drive your truck. I'll rent a station wagon and we can bring more refugees back that way."

"I'm leaving at four thirty in the morning," I say, trying to discourage him.

"I'll be here at four o'clock and will bring breakfast and coffee," he says.

And so it starts. What follows after his return to Canada is a whirlwind, long-distance courtship: daily phone calls, letters (sometimes two a day), and flowers without a special occasion. "Isn't it Wednesday?" he would say when queried. There are two more weekend visits from Montreal to Vienna spent in long discussions on all aspects of life. He tells me the story of his family's escape from Czechoslovakia and their odyssey through France, Spain, and Portugal, trying to keep ahead of German occupying forces. Eventually, they boarded a ship that was supposed to take them to the United States. They were refused at Ellis Island and the boat was directed to Canada, where they disembarked in Montreal on New Year's Day, 1942. The family settled there, and Tom's father became a successful businessman.

It becomes clear that we have similar attitudes about many things, but most importantly, and against all expectations, we are having a good time. I am impressed with his wide range of knowledge, his political acumen, and his commitment to family. Being distant relatives, familiar with my religious history, he and his family ignore my mother's obsessive insistence on my continued Catholicism. At his third visit in six weeks, he brings the ring. "What if I say no?" I ask. But he is unshakable in his convictions that we are meant to be together. "You are just as excited about this as I am," he says, and as he places the beautiful ring on my finger, I know that he is right.

Breaking up with Adolf is very difficult. I have really been in love with him for quite a while, but we both understand that we have no future together. We know that his parents' lingering pro-German sentiments and my mother's paranoia about supporters of the former Nazi regime would never go away. He encourages me to do what is best for my future. The last time we are together, we both cry and wish for a different solution that we know does not exist.

It was November 1956 when Tom and I met. We are married in March 1957 in Vienna in a civil ceremony. The reception is fairly small, mostly his relatives from Canada and my family. It takes place at the elegant Hotel Sacher, just around the corner from our apartment.

We leave Vienna that night for an extensive honeymoon. On the plane I am overcome by a familiar emotion. I am on my way to a new life, in a new country, among strangers, with a new husband whom I barely know. I am once more afraid of my future.

"Had it been possible for me to fix the plane permanently in the sky, to defy the winds and clouds and all the forces pushing it upward and pulling it earthward, I would have willingly done so. I would have stayed in my seat with my eyes closed, all strength and passion gone, my mind as quiescent as a coat rack under a forgotten hat, and I would have remained there, timeless, unmeasured, unjudged, bothering no one, suspended forever between my past and my future."

— JERZY KOSIŃSKI, *Steps*

SAG HARBOR

• Summer 2020 •

THIS LOVELY HISTORICAL VILLAGE in New York on the shores of Peconic Bay in eastern Long Island is where I live now and will probably stay until the end of my days, enjoying the view of the majestic ocean and the beauty and tranquility of the mostly authentic old houses dating back to the 1800s.

I came here for the first time in the late 1990s after I had moved to New York from Montreal and was looking for a weekend retreat nearby. I was working for an Israeli-based organization called AMCHA, dealing with the post-traumatic stress of Holocaust survivors—a long, long way from where I came from and a long, long way from what I used to feel like. Through my marriage to Tom, I acquired knowledge of Jewish society and recognized the power of Jewish organizations. Tom and his father were becoming very successful businessmen, and their philanthropic endeavors brought us to Israel, sometimes as often as twice a year.

Life in North America was organized around one's religious affiliation, which was a new experience for me. This did not exist in Europe. My interest and appreciation of the existence of organized Jewish society helped sustain me in my marriage. It gave me a sense of security and purpose. I often wondered if it would have made a difference in my life if similar structures existed in Europe before the onset of World War II. Today, I do not think so. But in those early years of my marriage, having a Jewish identity and playing an important role in Tom's philanthropic endeavors, I believed it. And at that time, it gave me an interesting and purposeful life. It afforded me the opportunity to meet some of the most important figures of the time: heads of state, prime ministers, giants of industry, and brilliant scientists from large corporations. I hosted many memorable dinners, cocktail parties, and fundraisers in a beautiful, big old house with many bedrooms for family and visitors. I developed a sterling reputation as a hostess.

Those were the good aspects of my life, but there were many serious problems too. My husband's parents, Holocaust survivors themselves, had their own difficulties. Their neuroses were not apparent to me in the early years of my marriage because they were so different from the ones I knew from my own family. In contrast to my mother, Tom's mother and father were full of praise about my achievements. They never raised their voices and were very appreciative of whatever I did. It was such a relief not to be criticized constantly by my mentally ill mother. When I decided not to practice medicine and devote myself to the family's needs, Tom's parents were thrilled with my decision.

I found it quaint at first to be expected to call my mother-in-law twice a day, or more seriously, to drive her everywhere. She would not leave her house to go anywhere alone. Initially, I did not recognize this as a serious problem for me or my marriage. Eventually, I came to recognize that spending lengthy vacations with my in-laws once or twice a year was not quaint but seriously flawed and interfered in my relationship with my husband. But by that time, I was the caretaker of everyone, often left alone with my mother-in-law and my children when Tom went on long business trips with his father.

When my third child was born, I was in my midthirties and miserable. I needed something to do to counteract my despair. Practicing medicine was out of the question. Besides, I was no longer interested in a medical career. Fortunately, my love of interiors and the example of my beautiful house, which I designed and decorated, gave me the opportunity to establish a successful career as an interior designer. For the first time in my life, I was earning money. Within two years, I was not only established but considered one of the top decorators in the city. I was doing it on my own and was having a life in addition to being a housewife and mother. I traveled to design shows in New York and Europe and bought antiques and furnishings for my clients all over the world. Eventually, I employed three people and made a profit. Meanwhile, my husband and I grew further and further apart. In spite of my professional success, I felt lonely and neglected, and a ten-year drinking spree started that contributed to my already faltering marriage.

When in 1984 I got sober, I realized that my business was on the way to failing and my marriage was crumbling. All attempts to revive either were in vain. My reputation was gone, and Tom was in a relationship with someone else. We separated, we tried to reconcile, and finally by the end of the 1980s we were divorced. As the former wife of one of the most successful Jewish leaders in Montreal, I discovered that it was his city, not mine. I dissolved what was left of my business and finalized my lifelong dream of living in New York. I bought a beautiful apartment in Manhattan. I had a great job with the nonprofit AMCHA.

Eventually, I started to spend my weekends in Sag Harbor, where I live now. I met and married a man seventeen years my senior, a Canadian World War II veteran fighter pilot. We had a very good sober life for a while, but unfortunately he died a number of years ago at the age of 93.

All these changes and new circumstances did not alter my problems with my mother. She chose to stay in Vienna, in spite of my frequent invitations for her to move to Canada and later New York, particularly after Pista died in 1984. Mother was increasingly out of control. She accused everyone of stealing from her and of wanting to do her harm. Her moderate drinking habit of earlier years was escalating and so was her pathological behavior. Mother barricaded herself in her apartment and all attempts to help her failed. She was very convincing and as skilled a manipulator of people as she had been during the war, when that ability often helped to save our lives. She convinced her doctors and her lawyers that Katika and I were visiting her just to rob her of her possessions and money. None of the professionals believed us when we told them about her drinking.

One day, Mother fell in her apartment and could not get up. It took her two days to crawl to the telephone. The fire department had to use ladders to go in through her balcony door because her front door was so seriously barricaded that they could not break it in. I received a call from her physician asking me to come to Vienna. Mother had broken her pelvis and was hospitalized. He admitted that he now believed that she was drinking, as she had tried to bribe two different cleaning ladies at the hospital to bring her bottles of wine.

"She is well enough to be discharged," the doctor said, "but she cannot go home or she will drink herself to death. Besides," he continued, "she also shows early signs of dementia. She should be supervised at home or in a sanitorium."

The doctor and I told Mother that we were taking her to a physical rehabilitation center where they would help her with her walking. In fact, I had secured a place for her in a fairly new Jewish old people's home, something that had never existed before in Vienna. It was expensive and very well run, and it worked. She was settled in a private room with her own furniture and pictures without too many objections. Helen, a woman whose husband was a patient in the same institution, became her full-time caretaker. A few months later during one of my frequent visits, it was obvious that she was well looked after and much better. She had no access to alcohol. She was given raspberry juice instead at Friday night dinners.

One day when I took her for a walk in her wheelchair and sat in the garden with her, she whispered, still afraid and ashamed to admit it, "I am so very comfortable here. Do you realize that everybody is Jewish?" I was more than surprised but had noticed lately that she had been agreeable, pleasant, and smiling at everyone. I had also noticed that people around her were becoming friendly and respectful toward her. The director told me that she, unlike some of the other people in the home, avoided confrontations. I had noticed that, but now in the garden I understood. She was Jewish again, surrounded by Jews, and felt safe.

On one of my subsequent visits, she said in a whisper, "I don't want to be buried in a Catholic cemetery in Vienna with Pista." I was surprised since she had a plot next to his and I had assumed that was where she wanted to be. "No," she repeated. "I do not want to be next to him and I do not want to be cremated." I did not know what to make out of this remark. "Who do you want to be buried next to?" I asked. But she did not answer.

I was convinced that she was thinking about my father, Henry. Her attitude toward my father since he had left for Australia had been unexplained anger, with accusations of neglect. She never missed an opportunity to say negative things about him. But I always knew that she never stopped loving him. I remember that early in my marriage, I decided I needed to find out for myself what my father was really like. At that time, I invited him for a visit to Montreal to see Marion, his first grandchild, and spend some time with us. The visit was a success. He got good marks from everyone, including Tom's very critical family. I too discovered that I really liked him. He was friendly, funny, emotionally open, and very pleasant company.

But Mother would not discuss the subject further and the dilemma was mine. I had no connection to the Jewish community in Vienna. The nursing home offered to help when the time came, but that did not seem right because I did not want her to be buried in the Jewish cemetery in Vienna either—where she had no relatives, no connection to anyone. I got in touch with the director of the Jewish cemetery in Budapest, where both her parents were buried, and after many discussions with him and the rabbi associated with the cemetery and a substantial down payment, I got special permission to bury her with her parents in their grave.

In February 1996, the call came from the nursing home that Mother had been taken to the hospital and her condition was grave. Katika, who was living in Brussels, Belgium, and I arranged to arrive and meet at the Vienna Airport the next morning. We went directly to the hospital. I was happy to see that Mother's private room was lovely. She acknowledged our presence and a few words were spoken. She died early the next morning. The nursing home in Vienna and the rabbi who arranged the transport of her body cooperated very well, and her body was soon on the way to the cemetery in Hungary, arriving within the twenty-four hours prescribed by Jewish law.

Later that day, Katika, Mother's caretaker Helen, and I took a train to Budapest about three and a half hours away. I was sad but also pleased that all of the carefully prearranged plans were working well. Tired, I closed my eyes and hoped to fall asleep, but Helen was asking me many questions about my last trip to Budapest, which I took in 1993 with my daughter, Marion. The purpose of the trip, both for Marion and me, was to verify the places and events I had been speaking and writing about. We called it the "roots trip" and had many memorable experiences.

Marion and I visited the still yellow church where Mother and I were baptized and the "designated house" in Budapest where I had lived with my family before we went into hiding. We found the house in Kisláng where we had lived as Christians. We found the roads we took to escape the German reoccupation, the Baltonkenese cave, and many other things I so vividly remembered. But the most memorable scene that came to my mind from that trip was the one that took place at the Dohány Utcai Synagogue in Budapest, famous for its intellectual life and its architecture. My grandfather Béla Ács was one of the elders there. I wanted to find some documentation of his role and maybe some paperwork about my family, including my parents' marriage certificate.

The doors to the temple were open when we arrived, but inside there was a disappointing surprise. An attendant sat at a desk in the entrance and informed us that we could not get into the sanctuary as it was under reconstruction. There was scaffolding everywhere for the ceiling repair, and the pews were covered with drop cloths and plastic to protect them. There were no workers around, only the attendant, who proceeded to tell us the arduous story of the reconstruction. While he spoke, Marion, unnoticed by the attendant, snuck into the sanctuary. I noticed her do it and I was glad that she was so interested. What I did not expect was a sudden piercing scream coming from inside, obviously from Marion. The attendant and I ran together inside, thinking that maybe she had tripped, broken a leg, fallen into an excavation hole, as many images of a possible accident quickly passed through my mind. While I searched for her among the scaffolding and the covered seats, I heard her call, "Here, look, here!"

I found Marion in the front sitting in the second row of seats, shaking and crying and pointing her finger at the nameplate in front of her. She was barely able to talk. I looked at the bronze plate and read "Ács Béla." She was sitting in my grandfather's seat. I too became extremely emotional. I was shaking too but all I said was, "How come? How did you end up here?" She said, "I didn't. I was looking up at the artwork in the ceiling. I saw one seat, not covered, and decided to sit down to look up more comfortably. When I sat down, I saw the name and realized that this was my great-grandfather's seat." She was crying now and so was I. Then she said, "How is it possible that among a few hundred seats in the sanctuary, the only one that was not covered that I could sit in was his?"

After I finished telling Helen the story, I write Mother's eulogy. I mentioned her suffering and losses but also her bravery and unconditional dedication to saving our lives. Her life was witness to the importance of luck, wit, courage, and even deceit in the service of survival. She was living proof not only of the damages of the war experience on the individual but also the difficulty of survivors to live a normal life again.

The next day, a small but important group of people stand around her graveside: me, Katika, Helen, a cousin named Rozsika, the rabbi, and a few old Hungarian friends. The Jewish burial ceremony is short and strangely satisfying to me, signifying a homecoming I never imagined would happen. We stood in front of the open grave and large headstone there since 1948 engraved with my grandparents' names: Ács Béla, Ács Adél. I visualize my mother's name, Georgina, on a smaller stone written in the Hungarian idiom, the way her parents and both her husbands called her: Gyorgyike.

The rabbi's parting words resonated with me for a long, long time: "May she rest in peace. May her memory be a blessing to all."